P9-DVA-735

A CULINARY COURSES JOURNEY

Princess Cruises gratefully acknowledges the hard work and dedication of its Food & Beverage department, with special thanks to Jonathan L. Wilson.

Additionally, we wish to recognize the significant contributions of the following:

DESIGN: G&O Design, Inc., Pasadena, CA

Gillian Gough, Creative Director/Designer • www.goughmarketingdesign.com

REVISIONS 2014: Gillian Gough, Gough Marketing Design

PHOTOGRAPHY: Kohler Studios, Pasadena, CA • Heinz Kohler, Photographer • Geannie Garcia, Photographic Assistant

FOOD STYLING: Victoria Granof

TRAVEL TEXT: Rick Gough

PRINTING: ColorGraphics, Los Angeles, CA

Les Lampert

BINDERY: BindTech, Inc., Nashville, TN

 ISBN 0-9718421-9-1

MAHL
CIAO

Exec Chef

PRINCESS CRUISES • 24200 Magic Mountain Parkway • Santa Clarita, CA 91355-1283 • 1 800 PRINCESS (774-6237) • www.princess.com

CONVERSION TABLE

DRY MEASURE

- 1 tablespoon = 3 teaspoons
- 1/4 cup = 4 tablespoons
- 1/3 cup = 5-1/3 tablespoons
- 1/2 cup = 8 tablespoons
- 2/3 cup = 10-2/3 tablespoons
- 3/4 cup = 12 tablespoons
- 1 cup = 16 tablespoons
- 1 cup = 48 teaspoons
- 1 pound = 16 ounces
- 1 bushel = 4 pecks

ABBREVIATIONS

Standard English

- cup = C
- fluid cup = fl C
- fluid ounce = fl oz
- fluid quart = fl qt
- foot = ft
- gallon = gal
- inch = in
- ounce = oz
- pint = pt
- pound = lb
- quart = qt
- tablespoon = T or Tbsp
- teaspoon = t or tsp
- yard = yd

Metric

- millimeter = mm
- centimeter = cm
- meter = m
- kilometer = km
- milliliter = mL
- liter = L
- milligram = mg
- gram = g
- kilogram = kg

WET MEASURE

- 1 tablespoon = 1/2 fluid ounce
- 1 jigger = 1-1/2 fluid ounces (3 tablespoons)
- 1 fluid cup = 8 fluid ounces
- 1 fluid cup = 1/2 pint
- 1 pint = 2 fluid cups
- 1 quart = 4 fluid cups
- 1 quart = 2 pints
- 1 gallon = 128 fluid ounces
- 1 gallon = 4 quarts
- 1 peck = 8 quarts
- 1 peck = 2 gallons

WEIGHT

- 1 ounce = 28.35 grams
- 1 pound = 453.59 grams
- 1 gram = 0.035 ounce
- 100 grams = 3.5 ounces
- 1000 grams = 2.2 pounds
- 1 kilogram = 35 ounces
- 1 kilogram = 2.2 pounds

UNUSUAL WEIGHTS & MEASURES

- 1 bit = 2 pinches
- 1 smidgen = 4 bits
- 1 dollop = 2 smidgens
- 1 gaggle = 3 dollops
- 1 gaggle = 2 glugs
- 1 blanket = 2 glugs
- 1 smothering = 3 blankets

VOLUME

- 1 milliliter = 1/5 teaspoon
- 1 milliliter = 0.03 fluid ounce
- 1 teaspoon = 5 milliliters
- 1 tablespoon = 15 milliliters
- 1 fluid ounce = 30 milliliters
- 1 fluid cup = 237 milliliters
- 1 quart = 947 milliliters
- 1 liter = 1000 milliliters
- 1 liter = 34 fluid ounces
- 1 liter = 4.2 cups
- 1 liter = 2.1 fluid pints
- 1 liter = 1.06 fluid quarts
- 1 liter = 0.26 gallon
- 1 gallon = 3.8 liters

TEMPERATURE

°C = (°F - 32) X 5/9

°F = (°C X 9/5) + 32

- 32°F = 0°C
- 40°F = 4°C
- 100°F = 38°C
- 200°F = 95°C
- 225°F = 105°C
- 250°F = 120°C
- 275°F = 135°C
- 300°F = 150°C
- 325°F = 160°C
- 350°F = 175°C
- 375°F = 190°C
- 400°F = 205°C
- 425°F = 220°C
- 450°F = 236°C
- 475°F = 245°C
- 500°F = 260°C

TABLE OF CONTENTS

ACKNOWLEDGEMENTS

FOREWORD 4

SAILAWAY 6
Caribbean

CAPTAIN'S WELCOME 26
Canada & New England

CANDLELIGHT 46
South America

CHEF'S 66
Panama Canal

FRENCH 86
Europe

ITALIAN TRATTORIA 108
Mediterranean

ALASKAN WILDERNESS 132
Alaska

CAPTAIN'S GALA 154
Australia & New Zealand

SOUTHWESTERN 176
Mexico

LANDFALL 196
Far East

BASIC RECIPES 217

INDEX 222

FOREWORD

COURSES: A Culinary Journey

As the sun greets her bow, the aroma of freshly brewed coffee fills the air and comfort is taken in knowing that the food and beverage staff has already brought this majestic Princess vessel to life. While our world sleeps, a devoted brigade of cooks, bakers and wait staff begins preparation for breakfast. Every new dawn heralds an exciting destination, as every meal promises another culinary journey. The service commitment made by the Princess professionals waiting to help you greet the day reflects their passion for culinary arts that defies a conventional definition of dedication. After all, there is a world of passengers out there to feed... and the days are short.

Surprises continue to effortlessly materialize as each meal is anxiously anticipated. Whether partaking in brunch at Sabatini's Trattoria, submerging into the Southwestern cuisine of the Painted Desert for lunch or marveling at the pizzaiola hand-tossing your favorite pie for an afternoon bite; the sights, sounds and flavors are more than just nourishing, they are life-enhancing experiences.

Across our Princess fleet of ships spanning the breadth of the globe, seasoned culinary craftsmen, who utilize only the best ingredients available, carry out their duties united with a belief that food is a collaboration between nature and chef, working best when altered as little as possible. This philosophy has enabled us to put together an ensemble of specialty dishes in combination with exactly the right amount of creative expression which allows passengers to experience one elusive freedom, captured only on a culinary journey at sea: choice.

In preparation for dinner, the Maîtres d'hôtel carefully study menus and create wine pairings while pastry chefs add delicate embellishments to the grand finale. Service excellence is more than just a part of our credo. It is a sentiment materialized in the gift of understanding that the smallest details are sometimes the most important attributes of individual attention, almost overwhelming the moment you step into the dining room. The atmosphere is rich with the culture and history of journeys past. The starched linens, polished silver and signature china set the stage for an evening of eloquence as a force of diverse wait staff performs with the authority of seasoned veterans. In this environment, dramatic results are achieved by heightening the dining experience of passengers — giving them far more than they ever dreamed.

The pages that follow are testament to the intense emotions inherent in soul-enriching culinary merit and distinction in service. The chapters conjure images of destinations and elaborate evening meals, reminiscent of the journey created by the courses our ships travel — and the courses composing each special menu. The recipes and pictures are designed to be guidelines for your own experimentation. Princess Cruises hopes that you will be inspired to continue the journey and share these new adventures and treasured memories with family and friends. Cooking is a labor which results in sharing, and sharing makes the effort worthwhile.

Alfredo Marzi
Master Chef

C.H.E.F.

A Culinary Heritage of Excellence in Food is the foundation upon which our passion for Modern Classical Cuisine is realized. Exceeding individual expectations commemorates a pinnacle of distinction achieved through Culinary and Service Arts.

CARIBBEAN

Journal – Caribbean

DAY 1 *Sail from San Juan*

It's late, around eleven o'clock. First, the bow edges away from the pier, then the stern. Slowly, she (this amazing ship) moves forward, gliding really, past the harbor entrance lights into the open sea. We're underway!

DAY 2 *At sea*

Settling in aboard this gleaming "Princess," enjoying her considerable luxuries and many comforts. Quick-moving pink coral clouds scud across the aquamarine sea. Dining decisions and activity choices similarly dot the ship's blue skies. Ship life has a rhythm unique unto itself. The fun is in learning to dance to it (even for those with two left feet).

Port of call, Barbados

It's just after 6 AM, the ship turns into Carlisle Bay. Bridgetown glows in the early morning back-light. There's a palpable excitement on board. Most everyone has a plan to explore.

The options are considerable: check out an old sugarcane plantation house (in the afternoon for tea); lunch at a local fishing villages (for pan-fried flying fish and plantains); wander the east coast scenic lookouts and beaches (to cool off in one of the coral-formed pools at Bathsheba); or stop in at a rum distillery – rum drinkers and sailors (yes, they're synonymous) will want to pay homage to the illustrious home of Mount Gay.

Port of call, St. Lucia

Over-night island hopping. A heaven-sent idea. Like purpley Zinfandel or dark chunks of semi-sweet chocolate. Fresh croissant, papaya and café au lait (for St. Lucia's 17th century French heritage) on the private balcony while the ship drops anchor off Pointe Seraphine. Music from a steel drum band playing somewhere on the beach wafts over the water like the musky perfume of a plumeria. Island choices sift down to a casual agenda of snorkeling and lunch, Creole family-style callaloo soup (spinach-like greens), curry and pepperpot stew. Thank heavens for the palate-cooling guava ice.

SAILAWAY DINNER

APPETIZERS

Caribbean Tiger Shrimp Cocktail
Mango-Tomatillo Salsa

Caramelized Onion and Bacon Tart
Fried Leek and Balsamic-Port Reduction

Radicchio, Endive and Butter Lettuce
Sun-Dried Tomato Vinaigrette

ENTRÉES

Conchiglie alla Campagnola
Lemon Chicken, Broccoli, Tomato, Olives and Garlic

Sautéed Filet of Zander
Herbed Couscous, Baby Bok Choy and Lemon Sauce

Slow-Roasted Prime Rib of Beef
Heirloom Tomatoes, Baked Potato and Natural Jus

DESSERTS

Classic Cheesecake
Strawberry Coulis

Profiteroles and Fresh Berries
Vanilla Cream and Leaf Tuile

DAY 5 *Port of call, St. Maarten*

A bit of a split personality here – two nations, one small island. The north is Saint Martin, the south Saint Maarten – one belongs to the French, the other to the Dutch. Long ago, it seems that the French and Dutch joined forces to fight the Spanish over this land, successfully drove them off (but didn't change the name the Spaniards gave the place), and then bickered with each other for decades over the placement of the border. In any case, St. Martin/St. Maarten is a delicious stop – conch dumplings, fried Johnny cakes, coconut shrimp and guavaberry coladas.

It turns out the island was inhabited by the Carib Indians – thus "Caribbean" – who were also cannibals (which makes the French/Dutch seem a little less...fussy).

DAY 6 *Port of call, Tortola*

Three facts: Tortola means "land of turtle doves"; it is also called "Chocolate City"; the adjacent island, is "Virgin Gorda" (fat virgin). This is a world painted in warm pastels, even former forts and sugar mills. The food is West Indies cuisine; turtle, spicy goat and curries of all kinds. The traditional drink of the British Navy, Pusser's Rum, is also served here, sometimes in a near lethal fruit punch described as a "Painkiller."

DAY 7 *Port of call, St. Thomas*

This morning we wake up as the ship slides past Green Cay and Hassel Island before settling in off St. Thomas' capital and only town, Charlotte Amalie. Market Square, once a slave market, is already full of local farmers selling tomatoes, squash, carrots and onions. All around, Danish red tile roofs, French rod iron and Spanish style verandas.

After a bit of shopping, a vitran (bus) tour of the town and the crystal white beaches of Magens Bay. Then, a chance to taste the Creole specialty "ole wife" and okra and cornmeal "fungi".

This evening, as the ship sets sail for San Juan, our return destination, a grand emotion floats above the promenade deck and lingers in the soft tradewind breeze. It is the same as when one has finished a truly wonderful meal but before one has left the table. It is the feeling of satiation and joy. A feast without end.

SERVICE EXCELLENCE

ANTICIPATING THE
SPECIFIC NEEDS AND
EXCEEDING THE PERSONAL
EXPECTATIONS OF NEARLY
20,000 GUESTS A DAY
... ACROSS THE FLEET
... AROUND THE WORLD
... DURING EVERY MEAL.

CARIBBEAN TIGER SHRIMP COCKTAIL

Mango-Tomatillo Salsa

Serves 6

24 jumbo tiger shrimp, peeled and deveined

COURT-BOUILLON

2 quarts water

2 lemons, halved

1 1/2 cups white wine

1 celery stalk

1 onion, quartered

10 white peppercorns

1 bay leaf

salt and pepper

SALSA

1 cup mango, small dice

3/4 cup tomatillo, small dice

1/4 cup red pepper, small dice

1/4 cup red onion, small dice

2 tablespoons chives, chopped

3 tablespoons white wine vinegar

1/4 cup extra virgin olive oil

1/4 teaspoon cayenne pepper, ground

salt and pepper

6 leaves iceberg lettuce, finely shredded

1 lemon, sliced

1 lime, sliced

The tomatillo, also known as the Mexican green tomato or the jamberry is a relative of both the tomato and the cape gooseberry. It resembles a small green tomato but is covered in a paper-like skin. Tomatillos should be purchased when firm and can be stored in the refrigerator for up to 3 weeks. Although popular in Mexican and Southwestern cuisine, the tomatillo's lemony taste also makes it well-suited for seafood.

Wash the shrimp, bring the ingredients for the court-bouillon to a boil, add the shrimp and poach for approximately 6 minutes or until just cooked. Do not overcook or the shrimp will become tough. Remove the shrimp from the bouillon and immediately chill well by plunging them into ice water. Remove from the ice water and drain. The court-bouillon can be reserved for future use.

Mix together all of the salsa ingredients and adjust the seasoning when mixed and again before serving. The salsa is best if mixed 30 minutes prior to serving and allowed to set so that the flavors can blend nicely. If you are preparing the salsa more than 30 minutes in advance, do not add the red onion until the last minute or the onion flavor may overpower the salsa.

Place the tiger shrimp and salsa over the shredded lettuce to serve and garnish with the lemon and lime slices.

CARAMELIZED ONION AND BACON TART

Fried Leek and Balsamic-Port Reduction

Serves 6

pâte brisée (p. 221)

TART FILLING

½ cup bacon, chopped

¼ cup red onions, small dice

1 teaspoon garlic, chopped

½ cup leeks, small dice

2 eggs

⅔ cup heavy cream

nutmeg, salt and pepper

PORT ONIONS

1½ cups pearl onions

3 tablespoons butter

3 tablespoons sugar

1 cup port wine

¼ cup balsamic vinegar

2 cups leeks, julienne

flour for dusting

vegetable oil for frying

salt

1 onion, sliced thick

butter for sautéing

Blind Baking is a method used to pre-bake pastry before it is filled without allowing it to rise or bubble. Most commonly the pastry is pricked with a fork. If holes are not desired, then the pastry can be lined with foil or parchment paper and filled with dried beans, uncooked rice or metal baking beads.

Roll the pâte brisée to a ¼-inch thick on a floured surface or between two sheets of parchment paper. Cut the dough into 5-inch circles with a ring cutter or a small knife and fill 6 buttered, 4-inch tart shells. Preheat the oven to 450°F and blind bake for 8 to 10 minutes until lightly browned. Remove the tarts from the oven and prepare the filling.

Sauté the bacon until browned, remove the excess oil and add the onion, garlic and leeks. Sauté until tender. Remove from heat and cool slightly. Add the egg, cream and seasoning and mix well. Divide equally between the tart shells and bake in a preheated 375°F oven for 6 to 8 minutes or until the egg sets.

To prepare the port onions, combine the onions, butter and sugar in a heavy bottom pan and cook until well caramelized. Add the port wine and balsamic vinegar and reduce to a light syrup. Onions should be tender and rich in color and aroma. The liquid will become the reduction.

Dust the leeks with flour and deep-fry in the vegetable oil until lightly browned. Place on an absorbent towel and season well with salt.

Sauté the thick onion slices in the butter over moderate heat until tender and well caramelized. Take care when turning the onion not to let the rings fall apart.

Top a warm tart with a caramelized onion slice, fried leeks and finish with the port onions and sauce.

RADICCHIO, ENDIVE & BUTTER LETTUCE

Sun-Dried Tomato Vinaigrette

Serves 6

SALAD

2 heads radicchio leaves

2 heads Belgian endive leaves

1 head butter lettuce leaves

1 bunch arugula

DRESSING

3/4 cup olive oil

juice from one lemon

1/4 cup balsamic vinegar

1/2 cup sun-dried tomatoes

1/4 cup tomato juice

1 tablespoon garlic, chopped

2 teaspoons Dijon mustard

dash Worcestershire sauce

dash Tabasco sauce

12 leaves fresh basil

salt and pepper

1/2 cup pine nuts, toasted

12 yellow baby pear tomatoes, halved

3 tablespoons green olives, pitted and segmented

3 tablespoons black cured olives, pitted and segmented

This salad combines the unique flavors of different lettuces such as the pepper spice of arugula, the pungency of radicchio, the bitterness of Belgian endive and the soft sweetness of butter lettuce. Any mixture of greens can be used. Be sure to select the freshest in season and create variation with color, texture and flavor.

Trim the lettuce leaves, wash the lettuces well in cold water and allow to drain between damp paper towels.

Combine all of the dressing ingredients in a food processor and blend until fairly smooth. A temporary emulsion should form. Adjust the seasoning and hold at room temperature. Stir the dressing well again before serving and adjust the seasoning again. The dressing should be made at least 30 minutes before use to allow the flavors to combine. Extra dressing can be refrigerated for future use.

Preheat oven to 300°F. Arrange pine nuts in a single layer on a baking tray and place in oven. Stir the nuts often and remove when they are just starting to turn brown as they will go from brown to burnt very quickly. The nuts will continue to brown once removed from the oven. Remove them from the hot baking tray immediately. They can also be toasted on top of the stove in a dry non-stick pan, tossing them continuously over moderate heat.

To serve, toss the lettuce leaves in a very light coating of the dressing and season lightly with salt and pepper. Arrange the leaves on plates and garnish with the pear tomato halves, the toasted pine nuts, the olive segments and more dressing.

CONCHIGLIE ALLA CAMPAGNOLA

Lemon Chicken, Broccoli, Tomato, Olives and Garlic

Serves 6

LEMON CHICKEN

1, 2-pound fresh chicken

2 lemons

1 bunch fresh sage

4 garlic cloves, crushed

salt and pepper

PASTA

1½ pounds dried pasta shells

1 teaspoon olive oil

2 tablespoons capers, chopped

2 teaspoons anchovy, chopped

½ cup cured black olives, pitted

3 cups fresh tomato sauce (p. 114)

2 cups lemon chicken meat

1 cup broccoli florets, steamed

chopped Italian parsley

Parmesan cheese

This recipe calls for the chicken to be trussed with butcher's string and roasted with the breast facing down. Trussing is a method of tying meat and poultry with string to create a uniform shape which promotes even cooking. The purpose of roasting the chicken breast down is to allow juices to flow into the breast during cooking as it is generally the dryer part of the chicken.

Preheat the oven to 425°F. Wash chicken well inside and out. Cut the lemons in half and squeeze the juice over the chicken and inside the cavity. Generously rub the inside and outside of the chicken with salt and pepper. Place the lemon halves, sage leaves and garlic cloves inside the cavity of the chicken. Truss with butcher's string and place in a roasting pan on a rack with the breast facing down. Put the chicken in the oven for 15 minutes and then reduce the temperature to 350°F and continue to roast for approximately 30 more minutes. The chicken is cooked when the juices run clear from the thigh. Remove the chicken from the oven and allow to cool enough to be handled. Remove all of the meat from the bones, pull the meat into fork size chunks and reserve in a bowl. Moisten the meat slightly with the lemon juice and drippings from the roasting pan.

Bring at least 6 quarts of salted water to a boil. Add the pasta and stir gently to prevent from sticking together. Boil until al dente, or until pasta offers a slight resistance when bitten into. Do not over cook, strain.

While boiling the pasta, heat the olive oil in a large sauté pan and sauté the capers, anchovy and olives. Add the tomato sauce, chicken and steamed broccoli florets and heat well. Add the pasta and toss until heated through. Adjust the seasoning and serve in a large bowl or plate topped with the fresh Italian parsley and shredded Parmesan cheese.

SAUTÉED FILET OF ZANDER

Herbed Couscous, Baby Bok Choy and Lemon Sauce

Serves 6

6, 7-ounce Zander filets, skin-on

COUSCOUS

1 1/4 cups fish stock (p. 220)
(chicken stock or water may be substituted)

1 tablespoon olive oil

1/4 cup onion, small dice

1/4 cup red pepper, small dice

1/4 cup cucumber, small dice

1 1/2 cups couscous

1 teaspoon fresh sage, chopped

1 teaspoon fresh parsley, chopped

1 fresh lemon, halved

salt and pepper

LEMON SAUCE

2 tablespoons onion, chopped

1 teaspoon garlic, chopped

1 sprig of parsley

4 white peppercorns

1 1/2 cups white wine

juice from two lemons

1 1/2 cups fish stock
(if not using fish stock, replace with more cream, not water)

2 cups heavy cream

salt and white pepper

12 stalks baby bok choy

1/2 teaspoon butter

salt and pepper

Zander is a firm and flaky white flesh fish harvested from the cold waters off of the coast of Russia and resembles a cross between a pike and an ocean perch. Any good quality saltwater or freshwater fish can be substituted.

To prepare the fish, score the skin side of the filets by making 3 or 4 shallow cuts in the surface. This will help prevent the filets from curling and will promote even cooking. Season well with salt and pepper. Place skin side down in a hot sauté pan with very little oil. Once the skin side has browned, turn the filets and brown the other side. Reduce heat and finish cooking until the flesh has slightly firmed and becomes opaque. Squeeze fresh lemon over the fish just before the filets are finished cooking. Do not over cook.

Meanwhile, bring the stock to a boil. In a small saucepan, sauté the onions, peppers and cucumber in a little olive oil until slightly tender. Add the couscous and the fish stock, cover and remove from the heat. Let stand for approximately 5 minutes, remove the lid, fluff with a fork and season with the salt, pepper and fresh herbs.

Wash and trim the stalk of the baby bok choy and then cut in half lengthwise. Steam very quickly, approximately 2 minutes, just until tender. Toss the bok choy in a little butter, salt and pepper before serving.

To prepare the sauce, combine the onion, garlic, parsley, peppercorn, white wine and lemon juice in a saucepan and bring to a boil. Reduce the heat and allow to simmer until the liquid has almost formed a syrup. Add the fish stock and reduce by half. Add the cream and reduce by half again or until the sauce has reached the desired consistency. Adjust the seasoning of the sauce and strain.

When serving, place a fish filet on a generous portion of the couscous. Garnish with the baby bok choy halves and place a small amount of sauce on the plate.

SLOW-ROASTED PRIME RIB OF BEEF

Heirloom Tomatoes, Baked Potato and Natural Jus

Serves 6

ROAST

7 pounds rib roast

2 cloves garlic

6 black peppercorns

1 bay leaf

1 small bunch fresh thyme

½ cup dry red wine

salt and pepper

TOMATOES

3 red vine-ripened tomatoes

3 yellow vine-ripened tomatoes

3 green vine-ripened tomatoes

2 tablespoons garlic, chopped

1 tablespoon fresh parsley, chopped

1 tablespoon fresh thyme, chopped

3 tablespoons olive oil

salt and pepper

POTATOES

6 large Idaho baking potatoes

1 tablespoon vegetable oil

salt

sour cream

chopped chives

bacon, chopped

horseradish cream (p. 217)

The term heirloom refers to produce that is grown from original seeds that have not been altered or affected by modern agriculture or man-made hybrids. Heirloom tomatoes have been naturally pollinated and are usually raised in an organic environment. These tomatoes are harvested ripe with firm plump flesh and are full of flavor.

Preheat the oven to 450°F. Trim the roast and tie it tightly with butcher's string. Rub with the garlic cloves. Heavily season the roast with a course salt and pepper and place on a rack in a roasting pan.

Place the roast in the oven for 20 minutes, then reduce the temperature to 250°F and continue to roast. After a total of 1½ hours, add the garlic cloves, peppercorns, bay leaf, fresh thyme and red wine to the juices in the bottom of the roasting pan. The roast is ready when the internal temperature has reached 130°F (for rare). This will take approximately 3 hours, total. Cook longer for well-done meat, but do not cook over 155°F or the meat will begin to toughen. If the liquid in the roasting pan becomes dry during cooking, add water to it a little at a time. Remove the roast from the oven and allow to stand in a warm place for at least 15 minutes before slicing and serving. While the roast is resting, remove all of the liquid from the bottom of the roasting pan and strain it into a saucepan. Reduce the sauce while taking some of the fat off of the top with a small ladle. Adjust the seasoning before serving.

Preheat broiler, cut the tomatoes in half and rub generously with the garlic, herbs, oil, salt and pepper. Place them on a tray and broil for approximately 4 minutes on each side. Turn off the broiler and allow them to sit in the hot oven until heated thoroughly and slightly tender.

Preheat the oven to 425°F. Wash and dry the potatoes. Rub with a thin layer of oil and season generously with salt. Do not poke holes in the potatoes or wrap them with aluminum foil. Place them on a baking tray and bake until the skin is golden and crisp and the inside is light and fluffy. This will take 50 minutes to over an hour depending on the size of the potato.

Serve the sliced roast with a potato topped with sour cream, chives and chopped bacon, three broiled tomato halves, jus and horseradish cream if so desired.

CLASSIC CHEESECAKE

Strawberry Coulis

Makes one 9-inch cake

GRAHAM CRACKER CRUST

1 $\frac{1}{2}$ cups graham cracker crumbs

$\frac{1}{4}$ cup confectioner's sugar

7 tablespoons unsalted butter, melted

1 teaspoon cinnamon

CHEESECAKE FILLING

2 pounds cream cheese

3 eggs

$\frac{1}{2}$ cup sugar

1 teaspoon fresh lemon juice

pinch salt

SOUR CREAM TOPPING

1 $\frac{1}{2}$ cups thick sour cream

2 tablespoons sugar

$\frac{1}{2}$ teaspoon fresh lemon juice

STRAWBERRY COULIS

2 cups fresh strawberries

3 tablespoons Grand Marnier liqueur

1 teaspoon fresh orange juice

1 teaspoon fresh lemon juice

fresh strawberries

The secret to slicing cheesecake neatly is to use a length of dental floss or fishing line instead of a knife to cut the cake. Hold the string in each hand, pull taut and draw it down through the cake. Repeat the process dividing the cake to create slices of the desired size.

Combine the crust ingredients and press into a 9-inch round cake pan using your hands to form an even layer across the bottom and sides of the pan. Chill the crust well for at least 1 hour before filling.

To prepare the filling, mix the cream cheese and eggs together until smooth using a machine with a paddle or by hand with a large spoon and then add the remaining ingredients and continue to blend until well-combined. The mixture should be smooth and soft, but should not be full of air.

Preheat the oven to 370°F. Pour the mixture into the chilled crust and bake for approximately 20 minutes. The cheesecake will be slightly soft in the middle, but should be hot all the way through. If the cake splits in the center, it is over baked. Remove the cake from the oven and allow to cool to room temperature.

Meanwhile, combine the sour cream, sugar and lemon juice for the topping.

Preheat the oven to 425°F. Spread the topping on the cooled cheesecake and smooth. Put the cake back into the oven for 6 to 8 minutes to just set the sour cream topping. The topping should not turn brown and will not set completely. Remove the cake from the oven. Allow to cool to room temperature again and then place in the refrigerator to chill.

To prepare the sauce, clean the strawberries, cut into pieces and marinate with the liqueur, orange and lemon juice. Blend until smooth in a food processor or blender, do not strain. Add a few drops of water if the sauce is too thick.

Garnish with fresh strawberries.

PROFITEROLES AND FRESH BERRIES

Vanilla Cream and Leaf Tuile

Serves 6

CHOUX PASTE

1 cup water

1/3 cup unsalted butter

1 cup flour, sifted

1/8 teaspoon salt

4 fresh eggs

PASTRY CREAM

1 1/2 cups whole milk

1 vanilla bean

1/2 cup sugar

1/4 cup flour

4 egg yolks

CARAMEL

1 cup sugar

1/4 cup water

dash of fresh lemon juice

BERRIES

1 pint fresh strawberries

1/2 pint fresh blueberries

1/2 pint fresh blackberries

1/2 pint fresh raspberries

1/4 cup Grand Marnier liqueur

1 teaspoon sugar

leaf tuile (p. 192)

fresh mint leaves

To prepare the pastry, bring the water and butter to a boil. Add the flour and salt all at once and stir vigorously with a wooden spoon. Reduce heat and continue to stir until the mixture is a smooth paste and pulls away from the side of the pan. Remove the pan from the heat and let cool slightly for approximately two minutes. Add the eggs one at a time to the mixture, stirring well to incorporate. The mixture should be smooth and stiff. Let cool to room temperature.

Preheat oven to 400°F. Place the mixture in a piping bag with a medium-sized tip. Pipe 18 small balls of mixture, about 1 inch in diameter, onto a buttered baking tray. Leave at least 2 inches of space in between each ball for expansion during baking. Place the tray in the oven at 400°F for 10 minutes, then reduce the temperature to 350°F and continue to bake 10 to 12 minutes. The profiteroles should be golden brown, dry and firm to the touch. Remove from the oven and allow to cool on a rack.

To prepare the pastry cream, bring the milk and vanilla bean just to the boiling point. Meanwhile, mix the sugar, flour and egg yolks together to form a smooth paste. Remove the vanilla bean from the milk and slowly mix the milk into the paste mixture. Return to the stove over a double boiler; do not boil. Scrape the seeds from the vanilla bean and add to the mixture. Continue cooking until it has thickened enough to heavily coat the back of a spoon. Remove from heat and continue to stir until cooled to room temperature.

Combine all caramel ingredients in a heavy saucepan, preferably copper. Bring the mixture to a simmer slowly over a moderate heat. Stir the mixture occasionally, but only until it is about to boil. Do not stir after this point or the mixture may crystallize. Use a pastry brush dipped in fresh water to wipe any sugar crystals from the inner sides of the pan while the sugar is cooking. The caramel should be removed from the heat when it has reached 320°F to 350°F. The sugar will continue to darken slightly upon standing. The sugar can be cooked longer if a dark caramel is preferred.

Working quickly, dip the tops of the profiteroles into the caramel and place caramel side up on a tray; allow to set. The caramel can be kept soft by warming in and out of the oven or over a water bath.

Cut the profiteroles in half using a serrated knife, creating a base and a top hat of caramel. Fill the profiteroles generously with the pastry cream using a spoon or a piping bag. Combine the berries, liqueur and sugar together to marinate slightly. Arrange three profiteroles on a plate and garnish generously with the mixed berries and mint leaves.

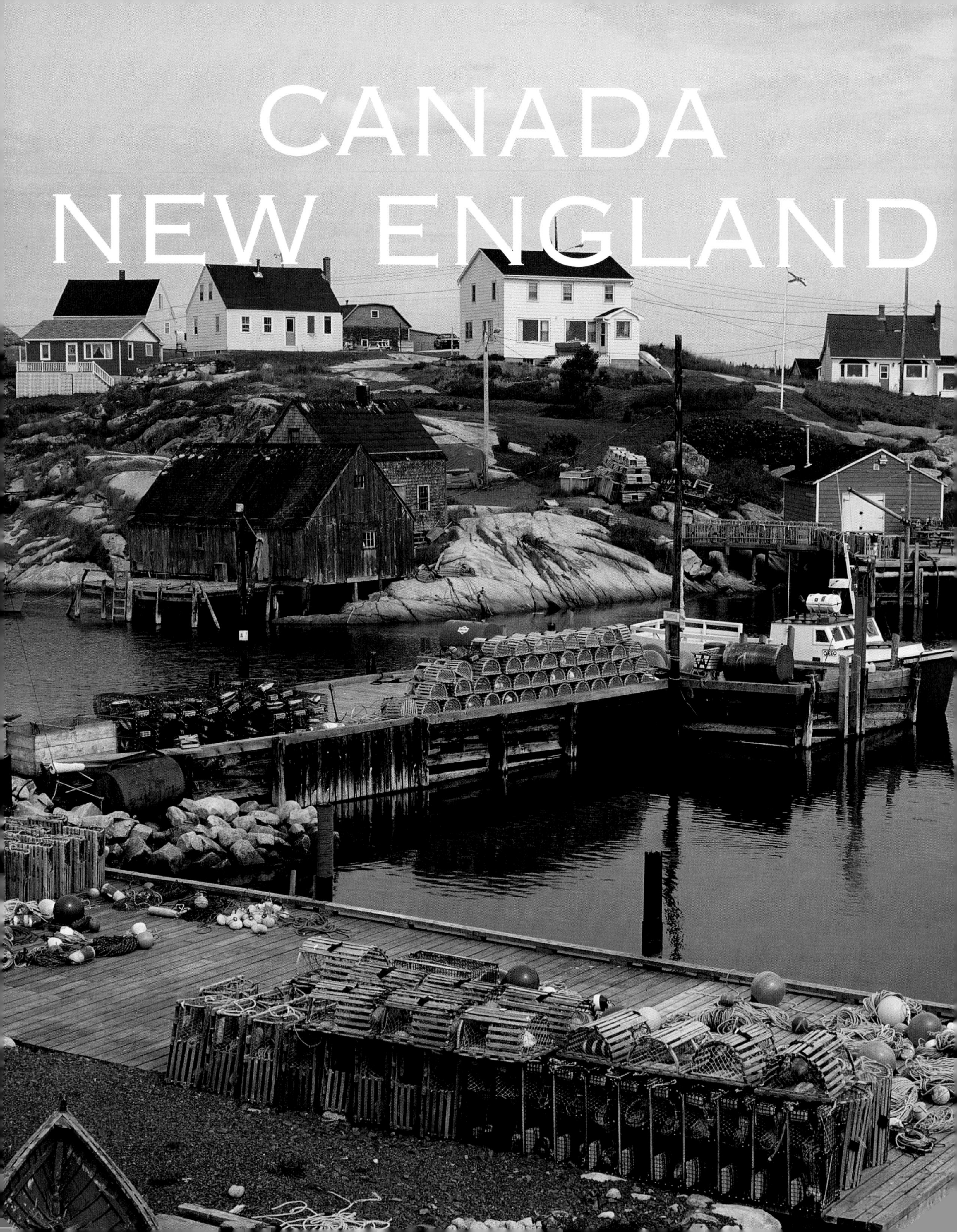

CANADA
NEW ENGLAND

Journal – Canada/New England

DAY 1 *Sail from New York*

A brisk Autumn breeze whisks the rust-red trees of the Palisades as the ship pushes into the Hudson current. Fall is definitely in the air. Heading north, following the march of history.

DAY 3 *Port of call, Halifax, Nova Scotia*

In early-morning fog, the ship makes her way up Eastern Passage past emblems of Nova Scotia's spirit: a solitary lighthouse, a rugged shoreline and as the sun suddenly appears, sparkling coves. The shore excursion includes the history of the French Acadians (who found their way to Louisiana to invent Cajun cooking, thank heavens).

DAY 4 *Port of call, St. John, New Brunswick*

Saint John, old city of fur traders, Revolutionary War British Loyalists, wood ship-builders and potash miners (half the world's supply).

DAY 5 *Port of call, Bar Harbor, Maine*

Waking up on the coast of Downeast Maine is like taking a boat ride through Yosemite. In 1875 (and now), a resort for those seeking to run a hand over the shiny surface of glacier-polished granite and breathe in the salty pine-soaked air.

DAY 6 *Port of call, Boston, Massachusetts*

Boston. Its obdurate personality born in the center of the American Revolution.

DAY 7 *Port of call, Newport, Rhode Island*

Most ship's travelers head for the shore boat to see the "Gilded Age" mansions and wander the back alleys of old Newport. For some however, it's a good day to kick back aboard the ship and hum the anthems of our heritage.

CAPTAIN'S WELCOME DINNER

APPETIZERS

Gently Smoked Supreme of Duck
Mesclun Greens, Cassis Vinaigrette

Crawfish Quiche
Jalapeño Chili Relish

Chilled Golden Delicious Apple and Peach Soup
Hint of Dark Rum and Mint

ENTRÉES

Farfalle alla Rustica
Tender Veal, Morel Mushrooms, Green Peas and Parmesan Cheese

Lobster Thermidor
Saffron Rice, Asparagus and a Dry Sherry Mousseline Gratin

Baked Flounder Parmentier
Thyme and Balsamic Beurre Noisette

Pan-Roasted Venison Loin
Braised Red Cabbage, Gaufrette Potatoes and Gooseberry Sauce

DESSERTS

Drambuie and Coconut Parfait
Licorice Papaya Sauce

Caramelized William Pear Tart
Blackberries, Almonds and Sauce Anglaise

GENTLY SMOKED SUPREME OF DUCK

Mesclun Greens, Cassis Vinaigrette

Serves 6

CASSIS VINAIGRETTE

1 cup sunflower seed or neutral oil

½ cup red wine vinegar

½ cup cassis liqueur

¼ cup grape juice

2 teaspoons Dijon mustard

juice from one fresh orange

salt and pepper

6, 6-ounce smoked duck breasts

3 cups mesclun greens

1 pound ruby champagne grapes

edible flowers

fresh cracked black pepper

Edible flowers are a great way to add color, texture and flavor, as well as improve the presentation of your food. They are generally used in cold salads, appetizers, soups, desserts and beverages, but some can be stuffed and deep-fried for hot presentations. The most commonly used flowers are marigolds, roses, nasturtiums, lilacs, daisies, mums and violas. Blossoming herbs and fruits such as chives, squash, almonds, peaches, plums, lavender, chamomile and lemons also produce great edible flowers.

For the vinaigrette, combine all ingredients and mix very well with a whisk or in a food processor or blender. Allow to marinate for approximately 30 minutes. Before serving, mix again and adjust the seasoning.

Trim the desired amount of fat off of the smoked duck breasts and with a sharp knife, slice very thin on an angle.

Wash the mesclun greens in cold water and drain between moist paper towels. Very lightly toss the greens with a little of the vinaigrette and season.

Arrange the greens, duck breast, small bunches of grapes and edible flowers on the plate. Garnish with a splash of the vinaigrette and fresh cracked black pepper.

CRAWFISH QUICHE

Jalapeño Chili Relish

Serves 6

pâte brisée (p. 221)

FILLING

½ cup onion, small dice

1 teaspoon butter

1 tablespoon fresh garlic, chopped

1½ cups freshwater crawfish tails

2 tablespoons fresh jalapeño, chopped

½ cup brandy

salt and pepper

1½ cups heavy cream

1 cup milk

4 eggs

⅛ teaspoon cayenne pepper

salt and pepper

½ cup shredded provolone cheese

JALAPEÑO RELISH

½ cup heavy cream

1 cup plain yogurt

juice from one lemon

¼ cup cucumber, small dice

⅛ cup jalapeño, chopped

⅛ teaspoon cayenne pepper

dash Worcestershire sauce

1 teaspoon fresh parsley, chopped

3 teaspoons fresh cilantro, chopped

salt and pepper

Quiche is a very versatile dish lending itself well to almost any filling and can be served hot or cold as a canapé, appetizer, with a salad or as an entrée.

Roll the dough to a ¼-inch thick on a floured surface or between two sheets of parchment paper. Lay the dough in a buttered 9-inch x 2-inch round pan and trim. Allow the shell to rest at least 30 minutes before blind baking. Preheat the oven to 450°F and blind bake for 8 to 10 minutes until lightly browned. Remove the shell from the oven and prepare the filling.

Sauté the onions in the butter until tender. Add the garlic and sauté for 2 minutes. Add the crawfish tails and jalapeño peppers and cook for 5 minutes. Add the brandy and reduce. Remove the mixture from the heat and cool. Adjust the seasoning carefully.

Combine the cream, milk, eggs and cayenne pepper together mixing well. Adjust the seasoning carefully.

Place the crab mixture into the pastry shell. Pour the egg custard over it and stir gently to ensure even distribution of the mix. Sprinkle the top with the cheese and press slightly so that the cheese falls into the liquid.

Preheat oven to 375°F. Place the quiche in the center of the oven and bake for 35 to 40 minutes. The quiche is ready when the center is set and the top is browned. Remove the quiche from the oven and allow to cool slightly while preparing the sauce.

Whip the cream to a medium peak and then fold in all other ingredients carefully until well blended. Adjust the seasoning and chill before serving.

Serve a warm slice of the quiche with a generous amount of sauce. Garnish the plate with finely diced and thin rings of various peppers.

CHILLED GOLDEN DELICIOUS APPLE AND PEACH SOUP

Hint of Dark Rum and Mint

Serves 6

SOUP

2 cups Golden Delicious apple, peeled, cored and chopped

1 cup apple juice or cider

2 cups peach, peeled

½ cup orange juice

1 cup plain yogurt

2 cups fresh cream

1 tablespoon honey

½ cup dark rum

cinnamon

nutmeg

2 Golden Delicious apples, quartered, peeled and shaped

2 peaches, peeled and diced

fresh mint

When in season, fresh peaches are always preferred. When peeling a peach, cut a small X in the bottom. Place the peach in boiling water for 1 to 1½ minutes. Remove the peach and place it into cold water to stop it from cooking. The skin can then be pulled off with a small knife. When working with apple garnishes, squeeze the juice from one lemon into 2 cups of water. After cutting the apple, place the pieces into the lemon-water for approximately 5 minutes. This will help prevent the apples from oxidizing and turning brown.

In a blender or food processor, puree the apples with the apple juice or cider until smooth. Set aside.

Separately, blend the peaches and the orange juice until smooth.

Reserve a small amount of the peach puree for garnish. Combine the remainder of the peach puree, apple puree, yogurt, cream, honey and rum. Mix well and season lightly with the cinnamon and nutmeg. Refrigerate well.

Serve the soup in a chilled bowl. Using a small ring, garnish with the diced peaches and top with shaped apples, mint leaf and drops of the peach puree. As a variation in presentation, the soup can be served in a dessert glass.

FARFALLE ALLA RUSTICA

Tender Veal, Morel Mushrooms, Green Peas and Parmesan Cheese

Serves 6

1½ pounds dried farfalle
(bowtie pasta)

2 tablespoons olive oil

¼ cup shallots, chopped

2 teaspoons garlic, chopped

1½ pounds veal scaloppini, julienne

8 ounces dried morel mushrooms

1 cup fresh petite sweet peas, blanched

1 teaspoon fresh sage, chopped

½ teaspoon fresh rosemary, chopped

¼ cup Marsala

1½ cups veal or chicken stock (p. 221)

1 cup demi-glace (p. 220)

1 cup fresh cream

salt and pepper

chopped Italian parsley

Parmesan cheese for grating

The very pungent aroma and flavor of morel mushrooms make them the key ingredient of this dish. Morels are typically purchased dry and are full of sand and must be rinsed in clean water repeatedly. Once cleaned, drain them and squeeze the water out with your hands or wrap them tightly in a kitchen towel. Leave the morel mushrooms whole unless they are very large, then split them in half. The stems of larger mushrooms may be tough. Morels are most suited to moist cooking methods.

Begin by soaking the morel mushrooms in warm water until re-hydrated and rinse until clean.

In a large sauté pan, heat the olive oil over moderate heat and sauté the shallots until just tender; add the garlic and sauté 1 minute more. Increase the heat and add the veal strips. Sauté quickly until lightly browned. Add the morel mushrooms and blanched sweet peas and continue to cook just until the veal meat is done, approximately 2 minutes. Add the Marsala and reduce. Add the chopped sage and rosemary. Add the stock and demi-glace and simmer for approximately 3 minutes. Add the fresh cream and simmer a few minutes more or until the sauce has slightly thickened and coats a spoon. Adjust the seasoning. Do not let the sauce boil or the veal will toughen and the cream may separate.

Meanwhile, bring at least 6 quarts of salted water to a boil. Add the pasta and stir gently to prevent from sticking together. Boil until al dente. Do not overcook, strain.

Drain the pasta and add it to the sauce all at once. Let the sauce and pasta simmer together for 2 minutes. Adjust the seasoning again.

Present the pasta on plates or in large pasta bowls and garnish with the chopped Italian parsley and freshly grated Parmesan cheese.

LOBSTER THERMIDOR

Saffron Rice, Asparagus and a Dry Sherry Mousseline Gratin

Serves 6

6, 1 to 1½ pound live Maine lobsters

THERMIDOR

2 tablespoons butter

½ cup onion, diced

1 teaspoon garlic, chopped

1 cup shiitake mushrooms, sliced

½ cup red peppers, diced

1 tablespoon chives, chopped

1 teaspoon French mustard

3 cups béchamel sauce (p. 217)

salt and pepper

MOUSSELINE

¼ cup fresh cream

¼ cup dry sherry

salt and pepper

RICE

6 threads saffron

1 tablespoon butter

¼ cup onion, chopped

1 cup basmati rice

½ bay leaf

2½ cups water, chicken or fish stock (p. 220)

salt and pepper

18 asparagus spears

1 teaspoon butter

salt and pepper

The lobsters need to be poached and the meat removed. This is a lot of work and can be done the morning or even the night before. In a very large pot bring enough heavily salted water to cover the lobsters to a boil. For presentation purposes the lobster tail needs to remain straight. To prevent it from curling when cooked you can either tie the lobster tail tightly to a board or you can insert bamboo skewers into the tail running from the end of the tail up to the body cavity.

Once the water is boiling, plunge the lobsters into the water and cook for approximately 8 minutes. Remove the lobsters from the water and run them under cold water or put them in ice water to stop the cooking process. The lobsters should be slightly undercooked at this stage.

Remove all of the meat from the lobster being careful to keep it in whole pieces. For each lobster you need one whole claw and 5 nice slices from the tail. The remaining tail meat, claw and knuckle meat can be combined and chopped into chunks. Reserve the shells to use as garnish.

To prepare the Thermidor filling, melt the butter in a large sauté pan. Gently sauté the onions until soft. Add the garlic and sauté for 2 minutes. Add the mushrooms and red peppers and sauté until tender. Add the chopped lobster meat and heat through. Add the chives, mustard and 2 cups of the béchamel sauce. The mixture should be rich and slightly thick. Adjust the seasoning.

To finish the lobster, fill the 6 shells from the lobster tails equally with the Thermidor mixture. Layer the slices of tail meat over the Thermidor mixture. Finish the mousseline by whipping the fresh cream to a stiff peak and then gently folding in the remaining 1 cup of béchamel and the sherry. Adjust the seasoning. Preheat the broiler. Lightly coat the filled tails with the mousseline sauce and place under the broiler until browned being careful not to dry out the lobster meat.

For the rice, begin by placing the saffron in the cold water or stock and allowing it to steep. Meanwhile, melt the butter in a saucepan. Sauté the onions until soft. Add the rice and sauté for 3 or 4 minutes; add the bay leaf, stock and the saffron liquid and bring to a boil. Reduce the heat, cover the pan and cook for approximately 20 minutes. The rice should be soft and moist when cooked. Remove the bay leaf and adjust the seasoning before serving.

Trim the asparagus spears to approximately 4 inches long. Steam the asparagus until just tender, but still crisp, approximately 4 minutes. Toss the spears in the butter, salt and pepper before serving.

Arrange the Thermidor on a bed of the saffron rice and serve with the asparagus. The head and tail shell pieces can be trimmed with kitchen sheers and used along with sprigs of watercress or other fresh herbs for garnish.

BAKED FLOUNDER PARMENTIER

Thyme and Balsamic Beurre Noisette

Serves 6

6 whole flounder, cleaned and skinned

butter for brushing

juice from one lemon

salt and pepper

duchesse potatoes (p. 171)

6 baby beets

6 baby carrots

36 sugar snap pea pods

BEURRE NOISETTE

4 tablespoons butter

juice from one lemon

¼ cup balsamic vinegar

1 teaspoon garlic, chopped

2 teaspoons fresh thyme, chopped

1½ cups demi-glace (p. 220)

salt and pepper

The flounder may also be substituted with a good quality sole. Both of these fish go from perfectly cooked to dry very quickly and require attention in their last few minutes of preparation to prevent that from happening. For ease of eating, once cooked, use a long thin spatula and carefully remove the top two filets from the bones. The bones can then be pulled off of the bottom filets in one motion. Place the top filets back over the bottom and continue to prepare.

Preheat oven to 325°F. Lay the flounder on a buttered sheet pan. Brush the filets generously with butter. Squeeze the lemon juice over the filets and season. Place in the preheated oven for approximately 12 to 14 minutes.

Once the flounder is baked, remove from the oven and turn the oven to broil. Place the duchesse potatoes in a piping bag and pipe a decorative line of the potatoes down the center of the filets. Drizzle the potatoes with butter and place under the broiler just until brown.

Meanwhile, prepare the vegetables. Trim the tops of the baby beets; do not peel. Trim and peel the baby carrots and string the sugar snap peas. In a small pan, place the baby beets in 3 cups of cold water and bring to a boil. Boil for approximately 8 minutes or until tender, strain. The easiest way to peel the beets is to use a kitchen towel or heavy duty paper towel and gently rub them in the towel. The peel should come off easily. The carrots and peas should be blanched separately in boiling salted water until just tender, but still crisp. Just before serving, split the carrots and beets in half and toss the vegetables together with a little butter, salt and pepper.

The timing is very important for the sauce and it should be prepared at the last minute. In a heavy bottom pan, brown the butter over a moderate heat, stirring the butter continuously so that it browns evenly. Once the butter has reached a caramel color, add the lemon juice and balsamic vinegar. This will shock the butter and stop it from browning; otherwise the butter will go from brown to burnt very quickly. Let the butter, lemon juice and vinegar mixture reduce by half. Add the garlic, thyme and demi-glace, bring to a boil and season. The sauce is a temporary emulsion and may separate as it sits. It should blend together nicely when returned to a boil.

To serve, mirror the plates with the sauce. Place a filet of the flounder in the center of the plate and arrange the vegetables around.

PAN-ROASTED VENISON LOIN

Braised Red Cabbage, Gaufrette Potatoes and Gooseberry Sauce

Serves 6

2, 2-pound venison loins
3 tablespoons vegetable oil
salt and pepper

MARINADE
2 cups red wine
½ cup red wine vinegar
½ cup olive oil
½ teaspoon dry mustard
2 bay leafs
1 clove
½ cinnamon stick
3 garlic cloves, crushed
6 juniper berries
6 black peppercorns

BRAISED RED CABBAGE
¼ cup bacon, chopped
1 medium onion, sliced
2 green apples, sliced
1 cup balsamic vinegar
½ cup sugar
1 head red cabbage
12 bay leafs
1 star anise
½ cinnamon stick
salt and pepper

GOOSEBERRY SAUCE
2 chopped shallots
2½ cups fresh gooseberries
½ cup white wine
1 bay leaf
2 cups demi-glace (p. 220)
salt and pepper

3 large potatoes
vegetable oil for frying

Begin by marinating the venison loins 8 hours to overnight. Combine all ingredients of the marinade. Place the venison in the marinade making sure it is submerged; refrigerate.

For the cabbage, sauté the bacon in a heavy bottom stock pot over moderate heat until the fat has rendered and the bacon begins to crisp. Add the onions and sauté until soft. Add the apples and sauté for 3 minutes; the apples do not need to be peeled. Add the vinegar and scrape the bottom of the pan to loosen anything that may be stuck to it. Add the sugar and stir. Reduce the heat and add the remaining ingredients. Cover and cook slowly. Once the cabbage has wilted, stir the mixture well, replace the cover and continue to braise 30 to 40 minutes more or until the cabbage is well-cooked and the flavors are well-combined. Taste the cabbage from time to time and make adjustments by adding or removing seasonings.

For the sauce, combine the shallots and 2 cups of the gooseberries with the white wine and bay leaf in a saucepan and reduce by half. Add the demi-glace and simmer gently for 20 minutes. Strain the sauce. Just before serving, cut the remaining gooseberries in half and add to the sauce as garnish. Heat thoroughly and adjust the seasoning.

Wash the potatoes (potatoes can be peeled or not) and cut the gaufrettes on a mandoline or with a crinkle cut knife. Alternatively, the potatoes can be cut into ¼-inch disks. Deep-fry the potatoes in vegetable oil until golden brown. Drain onto an absorbent towel and season generously with salt and pepper while still hot.

In a heavy sauté pan, heat the oil over a high heat. Meanwhile, remove the venison from the marinade and pat dry. Season generously with salt and pepper and sear on all sides in the hot oil. Reduce the heat moderately and continue to cook them in the pan, turning occasionally for approximately 6 minutes. Venison is best served rare. Overcooking will make it tough and dry. Once the venison is cooked as desired, remove it from the pan and allow it to rest on a cutting board for 7 to 10 minutes; slice.

Arrange the venison slices on a bed of braised red cabbage. Serve with the gaufrette potatoes and gooseberry sauce.

DRAMBUIE AND COCONUT PARFAIT

Licorice Papaya Sauce

Serves 6

PARFAIT

6 egg yolks

1 cup sugar

2/3 cup milk

2/3 cup smooth coconut milk

3 tablespoons Drambuie liqueur

1 1/2 cups fresh cream

SAUCE

2 1/2 cups papaya juice

1/2 cup light honey

1 teaspoon Drambuie liqueur

1/8 teaspoon anise essence

1/2 cup shredded coconut

2 kiwi, small dice

1 papaya, small dice

Although rich in flavor, parfaits are light and airy. They can be varied to include almost any flavor from fruit to alcohol to savory items. Parfait should be removed from the freezer a few minutes before serving and can be presented in many different shapes and molds.

Cream the egg yolks and sugar together gently without incorporating too much air. Meanwhile, bring the milk and coconut milk just to a boil. Slowly add the hot milk into the eggs and sugar mixture until it is well-combined. Add the Drambuie, return the mixture to a moderate heat and continue to cook until the custard thickens and coats the back of a spoon; do not boil the custard or it will curdle. Remove from the heat and cool. The custard can be put into a stand mixer and mixed on the lowest speed to prevent a film from forming on the surface while cooling.

Meanwhile, whip the cream to a stiff peak, but do not over whip or the flavor will become buttery. Gently fold the whipped cream into the cooled custard. Pour the parfait mix into the desired molds and freeze overnight. The parfait should not be made more than 24 hours before it will be served.

Prepare the sauce by simmering the papaya juice in a saucepan and reducing it by half. Mix in the honey, Drambuie and anise essence and let cool.

Preheat oven to 350°F. Spread the shredded coconut on a baking tray and toast in the oven stirring frequently for even toasting. Remove the coconut when just light brown as it will darken a little upon standing.

Un-mold the parfait by running cold water over the mold. Serve it with the papaya sauce and diced papaya and kiwi. Garnish with shredded coconut.

CARAMELIZED WILLIAM PEAR TART

Blackberries, Almonds and Sauce Anglaise

Serves 6

ALMOND CUSTARD
4 egg yolks

6 tablespoons cornstarch

½ cup sugar

1 vanilla bean

2 cups milk

1 cup ground almonds

POACHED PEARS
3 Williams pears

3 cups white wine

½ cup sugar

juice from one lemon

1 bay leaf

ANGLAISE SAUCE
6 egg yolks

½ cup sugar

1 vanilla bean

2½ cups milk

liquid from poached pears

3 frozen puff pastry sheets
(sheets can be purchased in the freezer section of your local supermarket and are usually 1-foot x 1-foot square)

1 whole egg

toasted almonds

blackberries

Make the almond custard by creaming the egg yolks, cornstarch and sugar together gently without incorporating too much air. Meanwhile, split and scoop out the vanilla bean, add to the milk and bring just to a boil. Slowly add the hot milk into the eggs and sugar mixture until it is well-combined. Return the mixture to a moderate heat and continue to cook until the custard thickens and coats the back of a spoon; do not boil the custard or it will curdle. Remove from the heat, strain and cool. The strained custard can be put into a stand mixer and mixed on the lowest speed to prevent a film from forming on the surface while cooling. Once cooled, mix in the ground almonds. The mixture will be stiff, especially once refrigerated.

Peel, halve and core the pears taking care to keep their shape. Place them in a saucepan with the wine, sugar, lemon juice and bay leaf. Gently poach the pears covered until they are tender, but do not cook them until they fall apart. Allow the pears to cool in the liquid, again, being careful not to over cook them. Remove the pear halves from the poaching liquid and let them drain. With a sharp knife, make slices in the pear halves starting 1 inch from the top and cutting through to the bottom to form a fan pattern. Generously sprinkle sugar over the fanned pear halves.

Prepare the anglaise sauce using the same method as the custard. If the sauce is too thick, thin it out slightly with the liquid from the poached pears.

Preheat oven to 425°F. Lay the puff pastry sheets out on the counter. Scramble the egg in a cup. Using a pastry brush, brush the puff pastry lightly and evenly with the egg. Using a sharp knife, cut out pear shapes from the pastry. The shapes should be a ½-inch larger on all sides than the pear half that will be placed on them.

Lay the puff pastry pears on a lightly greased baking tray. Spread a tablespoon full of the almond custard in the center of each pastry. Lay the pear half over the almond custard leaving room on all sides for the puff pastry to rise. Bake in the oven for 15 to 20 minutes or until the puff pastry is golden brown and the pear has caramelized.

Serve the pastries hot out of the oven with a generous portion of the anglaise sauce and garnish with toasted almonds and blackberries.

SOUTH AMERICA

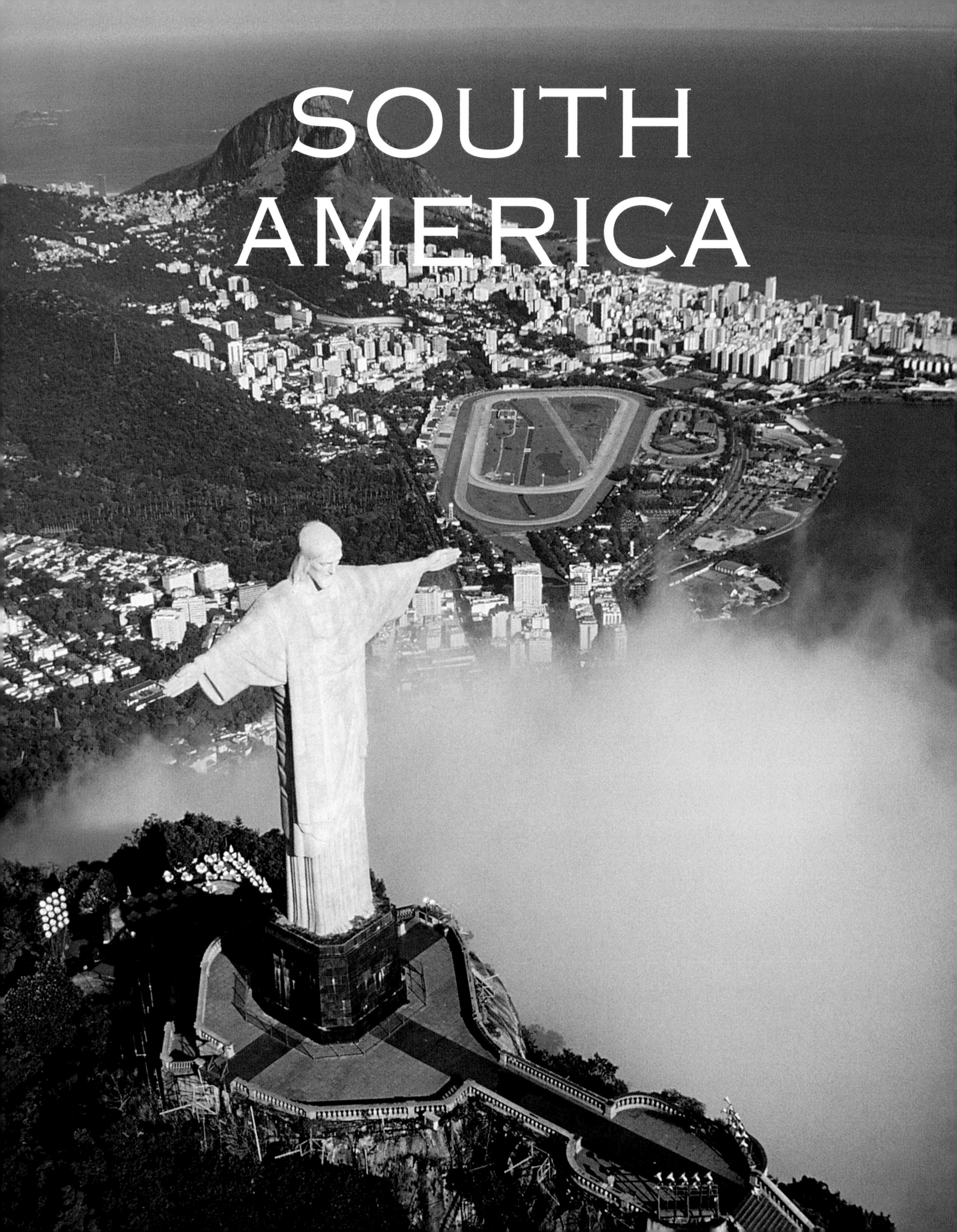

Journal – South America: Around Cape Horn, from Buenos Aires to Santiago

DAY 4 *Port of call, Puerto Madryn, Argentina*

The sun has just edged up into the southern Atlantic when the ship greets the bent tooth of Peninsula Valdez – in its shelter, Puerto Madryn. In only two days the cruise has traveled from the sophisticated big smoke of Buenos Aires to Patagonia, a land synonymous with "rugged" and "remote" (if that's not enough, it means "land of the big-footed people").

At Punta Delgada, we sit within scant yards of huge elephant seals, enormously basking in the summer sun, pushing their weight around for the best spot, or hunkering down to the shore for swim.

DAY 7 *Around the Horn*

The ship steams toward the most famous maritime landmark of all time. The names on the ship's chart are as telling as the area's reputation for gale-force winds and mountainous seas, False Cape Hope, Desolation Island, Hope Island, Deceit Island. Fortunately, the ship feels more like a "snug harbor."

When we finally arrive at the area in a relatively placid 30 knots of wind, the Cape (actually an island) is shrouded in mist, unwilling to give up its secrets. A fierce whirlwind suddenly blows across the archipelago and, for a few moments, the Horn appears across the boil of wind-whitened water. A rocky sphinx allowing a momentary glimpse into its fabled mystery. A pair of wandering albatrosses as witnesses.

DAY 8, 9 *Tierra del Fuego northward*

Glad to step on land, even if Magellan did name the place "land of fires." Andean condors, flightless steamer ducks and diving petrels abound. Lunch is a delicate seafood stew featuring the excellent local centolla (spider crab).

Cruising in Beagle Channel, sight after sight presents itself, sheer-cut mountains, sea lion islands, enormous glaciers – later a chunk of blue glacier ice chills our gin and tonics. Eventually we're at Punta Arenas, Chile's historic port facing the Strait of Magellan. Where one can't help but feel the tug of world exploration, adventure and sailing. Meanwhile, the ships company loads fresh local line fish for tonight's dinner.

CANDLELIGHT DINNER

APPETIZERS

Warm Grilled Chicken Supreme
Field Greens, Thyme and Citrus

Baked Clams Casino
Bacon, Bread Crumbs and Cabbage Slaw

Chilled Strawberry Cream Soup
Pink Peppercorn and Crème Fraîche

ENTRÉES

Crespelle Gratinate alla Valdostana
Crêpes Gratin with Ricotta, Fontina, Cream and Tomato

Seared Deep Sea Scallops
Herb Ratatouille and Potato Noisettes

Medallions of Veal Tenderloin
Roquefort Crust, Turnips and Anna Potatoes

DESSERTS

Chocolate Grand Marnier Cake
Delicate Cream, Raspberry Royale and Rich Frosting

Lemon Poppy Seed Bavaroise
Candied Lemon and Striped Sponge

WARM GRILLED CHICKEN SUPREME

Field Greens, Thyme and Citrus

Serves 6

6 half boneless chicken breasts

salt and pepper

CITRUS VINAIGRETTE

1 cup extra virgin olive oil

½ cup orange juice

½ cup grapefruit juice

½ cup champagne vinegar

1 teaspoon honey

¼ teaspoon English mustard

½ teaspoon fresh thyme, chopped

salt and pepper

1 head Belgian endive

1 head red oak leaf lettuce

1 head green oak leaf lettuce

1 bunch arugula

1 large English cucumber

1 small red pepper, julienne

6 spring onions

12 orange segments

12 grapefruit segments

fresh thyme

Vinaigrettes are simply temporary emulsions of oil and vinegar in an approximately 3:1 ratio. They can be made more unique by varying the types and combinations of oils and vinegar flavors. Herbs, spices, flavorings, juices, alcohol, mustards and just about any other ingredient imaginable may be added to these bases. Vinaigrettes should always be prepared in advance of their use to allow time for the flavors to develop, and should always be seasoned with salt and pepper. They can be used hot or cold as a dressing, sauce or marinade.

Prepare the vinaigrette by combining the oil, both juices, vinegar, honey, mustard and thyme together and season. Divide the vinaigrette into two equal parts. Reserve one part for the salad dressing and use the second part to marinate the chicken breasts for at least 4 hours.

Remove the chicken breasts from the marinade, season with salt and pepper and grill over an open flame until just cooked, approximately 12 minutes. The chicken can also be sautéed or baked in the oven. Let the chicken cool slightly.

Wash and separate all of the lettuce leaves. Using a slicer or a sharp knife, cut long thin slices from the English cucumber. Roll the cucumber slices into rings and fill them by arranging the lettuce leaves, strips of bell pepper and spring onion flower in them.

The spring onion garnish is made by cutting a 2-inch long piece out of the white of the onion. Using a small sharp knife, make slices from ½-inch from the end of the onion, down through the opposite end. Repeat the slice all the way around the spring onion. Place the cut onion in a small bowl of ice water for approximately 15 minutes and it will open into a flower.

Serve the chicken warm by slicing it and arranging it on a plate around the cucumber and lettuce. Garnish with the orange and grapefruit segments and fresh thyme. Drizzle the citrus vinaigrette around generously.

BAKED CLAMS CASINO

Bacon, Bread Crumbs and Cabbage Slaw

Serves 6

18, 2-inch little neck clams

court-bouillon (p. 10)

BREAD CRUMBS

3 tablespoons butter

¼ cup onion, chopped fine

2 cups bread crumbs

3 teaspoons fresh parsley, chopped

½ pound thick sliced smoked bacon

SLAW

2 cups white cabbage, finely shredded

2 cups red cabbage, finely shredded

¼ cup court-bouillon

1 teaspoon butter

ground caraway

salt and pepper

fresh parsley, chopped

A court-bouillon is an aromatic liquid used primarily to poach fish, shellfish and vegetables. It is especially appropriate if the item is to be served cold. The purpose of the liquid is to help impart mild flavors into traditionally bland items. The court-bouillon should always be used at poaching temperature, 190°F. Items that are to be served cold should be allowed to cool in the court-bouillon. This will take a little patience and practice to perfect the timing to avoid over cooking the items left in the liquid to cool.

Bring the court-bouillon to a boil. Add the clams and poach for approximately 4 minutes or just until the clams begin to open. Cool the clams in the court-bouillon.

Prepare the breadcrumbs by melting the butter in a sauté pan. Add the onions and cook until tender. Add the bread crumbs and parsley and sauté until golden brown. The breadcrumbs should be moist enough to just hold together if pressed. If the crumbs are too dry, add more melted butter. Adjust the seasoning.

Cook the bacon in strips until well-browned. Remove from heat and cut the strips into 1½-inch pieces.

Preheat oven to 300°F. Remove the clams from the court-bouillon. Remove the top shell from the clams and remove the muscle from the bottom shell. Fill the bottom shell with a mound of bread crumbs. Place a piece of bacon over the bread crumbs and a piece of clam meat on top of the bacon. Moisten the clam meat with a little court-bouillon. Place the clams on a baking tray and warm in the oven for approximately 4 to 6 minutes. Be careful not to dry out the clam meat.

Meanwhile, lightly poach the white and red cabbage separately in a little bit of the court-bouillon for approximately 5 minutes or until just tender. If you cook them together, the red cabbage will turn everything purple. Keep warm. Just before serving, mix the two together and toss with the butter, caraway, salt and pepper.

Serve three baked clams on a bed of the cabbage and garnish with chopped fresh parsley.

CHILLED STRAWBERRY CREAM SOUP

Pink Peppercorn and Crème Fraîche

Serves 6 to 8

SOUP

4 cups fresh strawberries

1 cup white grape juice

1 cup plain yogurt

1¼ cups fresh cream

1 tablespoon honey

¼ cup Frangelico

1 teaspoon pink peppercorns

nutmeg

12 large strawberries, sliced

½ cup crème fraîche

edible flowers

pink peppercorns

fresh mint

Soups were once considered complete meals. Now variations, seasonal influences, cultural practices and eating trends have turned soup into a course generally served at or near the beginning of a meal. An addition to the classic preparations, chilled varieties of soups lend an unexpected twist to a meal. Chilled soups are easy to prepare and allow for creativity and experimentation. Any basic fruit, vegetable or meat item can be turned into a refreshing chilled soup. Chilled soups are especially nice for a hot summer lunch or even as a dessert when something a little less sweet is desired.

In a blender or food processor puree the strawberries with the grape juice. Set aside ½ cup of the puree to use as garnish. Add the remainder of the soup ingredients and puree. Adjust the seasoning and chill well. Adjust the seasoning again before serving.

Serve the soup in a chilled bowl. Use a ring mold to arrange the sliced strawberries in the center of the bowl. Fill the strawberry ring with crème fraîche. Pour the soup into the bowls and garnish with drops of the reserved strawberry puree and more crème fraîche. Finish garnishing with edible flowers, pink peppercorns and fresh mint.

CRESPELLE GRATINATE ALLA VALDOSTANA

Crêpes Gratin with Ricotta, Fontina, Cream and Tomato

Serves 6

CRÊPES

¾ cup flour

½ teaspoon salt

1 teaspoon baking powder

2 eggs

1 cup milk

2 tablespoons melted butter

vegetable oil for cooking

FILLING

1 tablespoon olive oil

½ cup onion, chopped

2 tablespoons garlic, chopped

2 cups fresh spinach, chopped

2 eggs

¼ cup Parmesan cheese, grated

½ cup fontina cheese, shredded

2 cups ricotta cheese

nutmeg, salt and pepper

3 cups béchamel sauce (p. 217)

2 cups cooked rich tomato sauce (p. 217)

½ cup basil pesto (p. 74)

fresh basil buds

Crêpes can be prepared in advance and then refrigerated for 1 to 2 days or frozen for up to a month. When refrigerating, wrap in a stack tightly with plastic wrap to prevent them from drying out. If freezing, put a piece of parchment paper or plastic wrap in between each crêpe and wrap the stack tightly. Thaw in the refrigerator. Unwrap once the crêpes have thawed, not before.

Prepare the crêpes by sifting the dry ingredients together. In a bowl, whisk the eggs and milk together. Add the wet ingredients into the dry, whisking well to remove lumps. The batter should be fairly thin. Drizzle and whisk the melted butter into the batter and chill for one hour.

Heat a 6-inch non-stick pan. Add a few drops of oil to the pan. Add approximately 2 ounces of batter, tipping the sauté pan to allow the batter to form a thin layer evenly over the surface. Continue to cook over moderate heat until the crêpe is lightly browned on the bottom. Carefully turn the crêpe over and brown the other side. Remove onto a paper towel to cool and continue to cook the rest of the crêpes.

Prepare the filling by heating the olive oil in a sauté pan. Add the onions and sauté until tender. Add the garlic and sauté 2 minutes more. Add the chopped spinach and sauté until dry. Season lightly and remove from the heat. In a bowl, combine the spinach mixture with the eggs, Parmesan, fontina and ricotta and season with the nutmeg, salt and pepper.

Preheat a 375°F oven. Lay out the crêpes. Divide the filling evenly between the crêpes and spread it out over their surface. Roll the crêpes up, forming roulades. Lay the roulades in a greased oven-safe casserole. Spread the béchamel sauce over the surface of the crêpes and bake in the oven for 35 to 40 minutes or until they are hot in the center and the béchamel sauce has browned.

Heat the tomato sauce on the stove.

Remove the crêpes from the casserole and cut them each into two or three pieces on an angle.

Arrange the crêpe pieces on a plate with the béchamel and tomato sauces around. Drizzle the plate with basil pesto and fresh basil buds for garnish.

SEARED DEEP SEA SCALLOPS

Herb Ratatouille and Potato Noisettes

Serves 6

36 large sea scallops

salt and pepper

vegetable oil for searing

1 lemon, halved

RATATOUILLE

½ cup olive oil

½ cup onion, large dice

4 garlic cloves, chopped

1 red bell pepper, large dice

1 green bell pepper, large dice

1 yellow bell pepper, large dice

1 cup zucchini, large dice

¾ cup eggplant, large dice

½ cup black cured olives, pitted

2 cups tomato concassé

2 tablespoons tomato paste

½ teaspoon rosemary, chopped

1 teaspoon oregano, chopped

½ teaspoon thyme, chopped

½ cinnamon stick

¼ teaspoon cayenne pepper

3 bay leaves

salt and pepper

3 large potatoes

chopped fresh parsley

Although the base for a ratatouille, or vegetable stew, does not change, the outcome can be varied greatly by the introduction of unique ingredients such as olives or capers along with the use and combination of various spices such as cinnamon and cayenne pepper. Variations should be used subtly. Ratatouille can be served hot or cold as a side dish, appetizer or vegetarian main dish.

Prepare the ratatouille by heating the olive oil in a large heavy pan over high heat. Add the onions and sauté. Add the garlic and peppers and sauté 4 minutes more. Add the remaining ingredients and stir well. Reduce the heat, cover and stew. Check the seasoning after 15 minutes and adjust (the cinnamon stick may need to be removed at this stage). Continue to cook for approximately 15 minutes more or until all of the vegetables are tender and the flavors have combined well.

Meanwhile, peel the potatoes and cut into quarters. Using a small sharp knife, shape the potato quarters to resemble Brazil nuts. Place the potato noisettes in a small pan, cover with salted water and bring to a boil. Reduce to a simmer and cook until the potatoes are tender, approximately 12 minutes. Drain and season.

In a sauté pan, heat a few tablespoons of oil over a high heat. Season the scallops well with salt and pepper. Sear the scallops on both sides until well-browned. Reduce the heat moderately and continue to cook until the scallops are just cooked, approximately 6 minutes. Squeeze the fresh lemon juice over the scallops when done. The scallops should be plump and juicy when cooked. If over cooked, they will become dry and tough.

Serve the scallops with the ratatouille and potato noisettes and garnish generously with chopped fresh parsley.

WE STORE 3 TONS OF ICE TO CARVE AS MANY AS 20 SCULPTURES DURING A CRUISE.

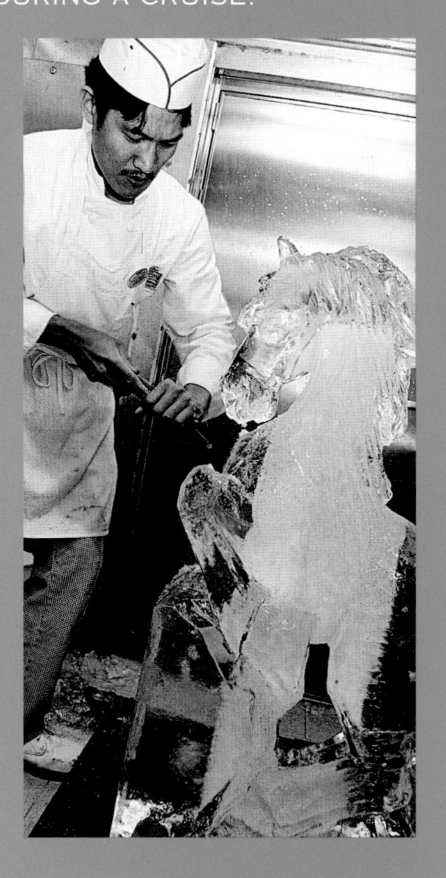

MEDALLIONS OF VEAL TENDERLOIN

Roquefort Crust, Turnips and Anna Potatoes

Serves 6

18, 2-ounce veal medallions

3 tablespoons vegetable oil for searing

salt and pepper

ROQUEFORT CRUST

1½ cups Roquefort cheese

½ cup fresh cream

2 teaspoons French mustard

2 egg yolks

salt and pepper

ANNA POTATOES

3 large potatoes

vegetable oil for frying

salt and pepper

1 teaspoon butter

3 teaspoons shallots, chopped

18 turnip wedges, peeled

½ cup brandy

3 cups veal stock (p. 221)

18 asparagus spears

½ teaspoon butter

salt and pepper

Blue, or veined cheeses are generally known for their bold flavor and pungent aroma. Most major cheese producing countries are recognized for at least one of their specialty blues: Roquefort from France, Stilton and Blue Cheshire from England, Gorgonzola from Italy, Bavarian from Germany and Mycella from Holland.

Combine the Roquefort, cream, mustard, egg yolks and seasoning for the veal crust.

Preheat oven to 400°F. Working quickly, peel the potatoes and shape them until they form cylinders. Using a slicer, mandoline or a sharp knife, make very thin slices from the potato cylinders (do not place the potato slices in water). Layer the potato slices in a small circle in a non-stick pan. Drizzle a teaspoon of oil around the perimeter of the potatoes. Place the pan on moderate heat with a little oil in the bottom. Cook until the bottom of the Anna potato is browned. Turn the potato over and continue to cook until crisp and browned.

Repeat this process until you have 6 Anna potatoes. The prepared potatoes can be re-warmed in the oven before serving. Season with salt and pepper.

In a heavy sauté pan, heat the oil over high heat. Generously season the veal medallions and sear on both sides until well-browned. Remove from the pan and place on a sheet pan. Spread the Roquefort crust over the top of each medallion.

Place the veal medallions in the oven to finish cooking for approximately 12 to 15 minutes. Just before the veal is ready to be removed, turn the oven to broil in order to brown the Roquefort crust.

Meanwhile, add the teaspoon of butter to the sauté pan that the veal was seared in, stirring to scrape all of the bits off of the bottom of the pan. Add the shallots and sauté. Add the turnips and brown lightly. Add the brandy and again scrape the bottom of the pan. Be careful not to burn yourself if the brandy flames. Reduce the brandy until dry and then add the veal stock. Simmer until the turnips are tender. Remove the turnips and continue to simmer until the stock has reduced by half and has thickened slightly. Adjust the seasoning and keep warm.

Steam or blanch the asparagus spears in salted water until just tender and still crisp, approximately 4 minutes. Toss with butter, salt and pepper before serving.

Make a ring of sauce on the plates. Arrange the veal medallions, turnips and asparagus in alternating positions. Place the Anna potato in the center.

CHOCOLATE GRAND MARNIER CAKE

Delicate Cream, Raspberry Royale and Rich Frosting

Makes one 9-inch cake

chocolate sponge (p. 84)

ROYALE (JELLY ROLL) SPONGE

8 egg yolks

1/2 cup sugar

4 egg whites

grated rind of 1 orange

1/8 teaspoon salt

3/4 cup flour

1/4 cup cornstarch

1 1/2 cups raspberry jelly

GRAND MARNIER MOUSSE

4 egg yolks

1/2 cup sugar

1 cup milk

zest and juice from 1 orange

1/4 cup Grand Marnier liqueur

3 leaves unflavored gelatin

1 1/2 cups fresh cream

chocolate ganache (p. 218)

1 tablespoon Grand Marnier liqueur

orange segments

chocolate garnish

Begin by preparing the chocolate sponge. Once baked and cooled, remove the cake from the pan and split into three layers using a serrated knife. Two layers will be used for this recipe; the third layer can be tightly wrapped and kept in the refrigerator for up to a week for future use.

Preheat oven to 350°F. Prepare the sponge for the jelly roll. Cream the egg yolks and sugar together. Whip the egg whites to a stiff peak. Gently fold in the egg yolk mixture and the orange zest. Sift the dry ingredients together and gently fold in. Line a baking tray with parchment paper and spread the mixture out evenly to a 1/4-inch thickness. Bake for 8 to 10 minutes. The sponge should not become too brown, or dry out. Once baked, turn the sponge over onto a damp kitchen cloth. Peel off the parchment paper and spread the jelly out evenly in a thin layer over the sponge while it is still warm. The jelly can also be slightly warmed if it is difficult to spread. Roll up the sponge to form the royale. For this recipe, you want the roll to be approximately 1 1/2 inches in diameter. You may need to cut the sheet of sponge in half and make two jelly rolls so that the roll does not become too large.

Prepare the mousse by creaming the eggs and sugar together. Separately, bring the milk, juice, zest and liqueur to a boil. Slowly whisk the hot milk into the eggs and sugar. Return to the stove and cook without boiling until the mixture thickens and coats the spoon. Meanwhile, soak the gelatin in a small amount of cold water. Once soft, squeeze out the excess water and dissolve the gelatin in the warm custard. Let the custard cool to room temperature. Whip the cream to a stiff peak. Gently fold the cream and the custard together.

Begin assembling the cake. Place one layer of the chocolate sponge in the bottom of a springform cake pan. Lay the jelly roll in a circle in the cake pan. Fill around and cover the jelly roll with the Grand Marnier mousse. Top the cake off with the second layer of chocolate sponge pressing firmly to ensure even distribution of the mousse. Cover the cake with plastic wrap and refrigerate at least 4 hours to set.

While the mousse sets, prepare the ganache recipe as listed with the addition of the tablespoon of Grand Marnier.

Remove the cake from the refrigerator and unwrap. Pour a layer of the ganache on top of the cake and form small peaks in the ganache with the back of a spoon. The ganache will set as it cools. Once the entire cake is well set, remove the springform and slice as desired. Serve it with orange segments and chocolate pieces for garnish.

LEMON POPPY SEED BAVAROISE

Candied Lemon and Striped Sponge

Serves 6

½ recipe chocolate sponge (p. 84)

½ recipe vanilla sponge (p. 150)

LEMON MOUSSE

3 egg yolks

¼ cup sugar

1 cup milk

zest and juice from 3 lemons

1½ tablespoons poppy seeds

2 leaves unflavored gelatin

½ cup fresh cream

CANDIED ZEST

zest from 6 lemons

2 cups water

¼ cup water

½ cup sugar

Preheat oven to 350°F. Begin by preparing half recipes of the chocolate and vanilla sponge. Prepare two piping bags with small plain tips. Fill one bag with chocolate sponge mix and the other with the vanilla. Line a baking tray with parchment paper. With a steady hand, draw alternating brown and white lines with the sponge mixes. Do not worry about making the edges neat because these will be trimmed later. Once the tray is covered, bake for 8 to 10 minutes being careful not to brown too much or dry out the sponge. Once baked, turn the sponge over onto a damp kitchen towel. Carefully peel off the parchment paper and let cool. Once cooled, keep covered so that it does not dry out.

Prepare the bavaroise by creaming the eggs and sugar together. Separately, bring the milk, juice, zest and poppy seeds to a boil. Slowly whisk the hot milk into the eggs and sugar. Return to the stove and cook without boiling until the mixture thickens and coats the spoon. Meanwhile, soak the gelatin in a small amount of cold water. Once soft, squeeze out the excess water and dissolve the gelatin in the warm custard. Let the custard cool to room temperature. Whip the cream to a stiff peak. Gently fold the cream and the custard together.

Line the inside of 6, ½-cup ramekin dishes with a strip of parchment paper. Cut the paper so that it sticks out of the ramekin approximately 1 inch. Cut the striped sponge to line the inside of the ramekins, but not so that the sponge sticks out like the parchment paper. Use a ring cutter or a small knife to cut a circle of sponge to go in the bottom of the ramekin. Fill the lined ramekins with the bavaroise up to the top of the parchment paper being careful not to leave any air gaps in the filling. Refrigerate for at least 2 hours to set the bavaroise.

Using a small, sharp knife, remove the zest from the lemons making the longest strips possible. Place the zest in the 2 cups of water and bring to a boil slowly. Drain the zest. This process removes some of the bitterness and softens the strips slightly. Return the zest to the stove with the ¼ cup of water and the sugar. Boil over a moderate heat until the liquid is absorbed being careful not to burn the sugar. Remove the zest and lay the strips out on a parchment paper-lined sheet pan to cool.

Once the bavaroise are set, carefully remove them from the ramekin. Remove the parchment paper and serve with the candied lemon zest.

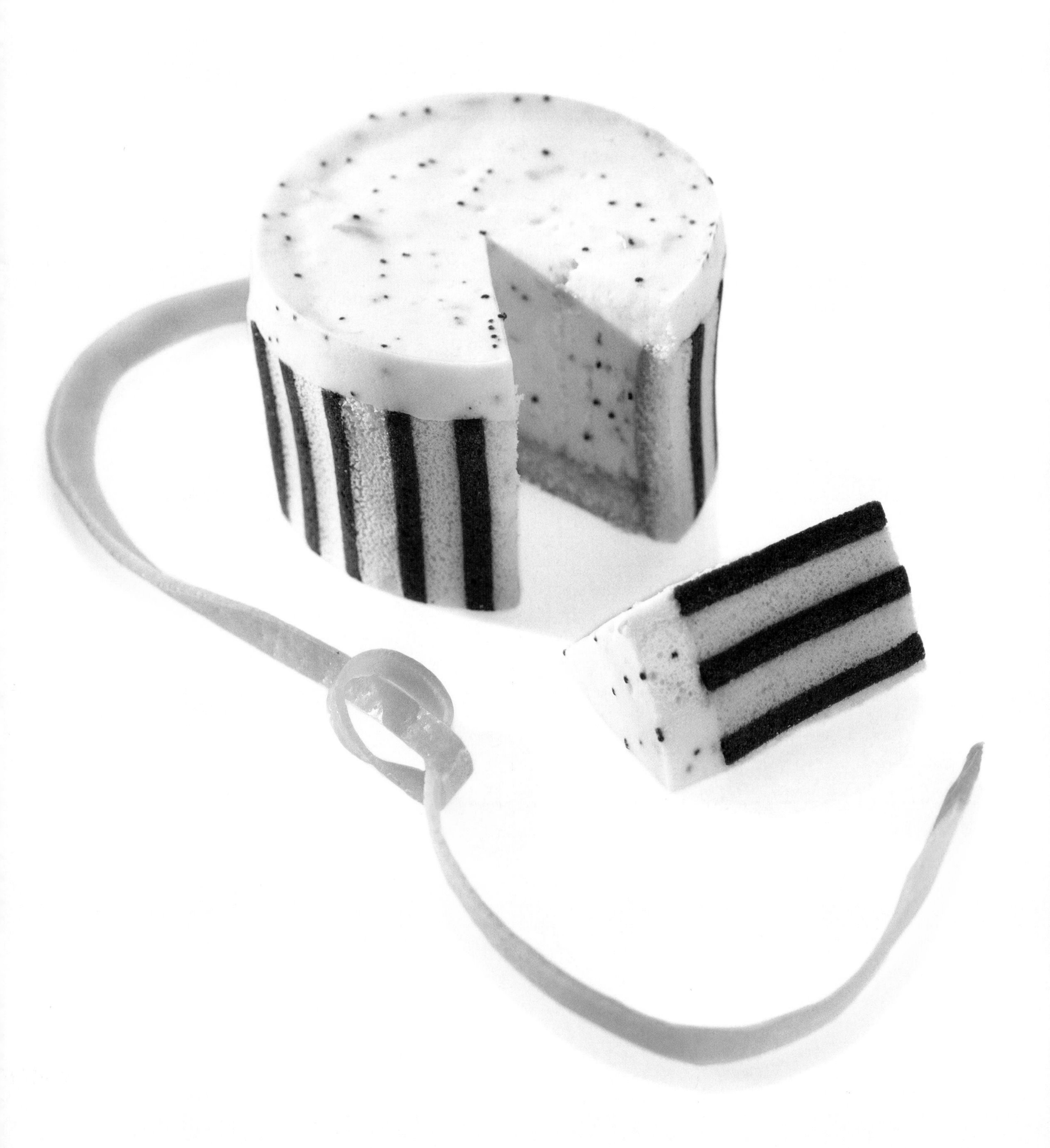

PANAMA CANAL

DAY 9 *Port of call, Huatulco, Mexico*

The Pacific Ocean is steel blue; the sky, pale navy; the air, Mediterranean soft. The ship turns the corner at Puerto Angel on the Oaxacan coast into the far-reaching Golfo de Tehuantepec. By days, we're about halfway between Vancouver and Ft. Lauderdale.

By the time breakfasts have been finished and morning strolls/jogs/meditations taken, the ship has anchored off Huatulco. At every turn there are white beaches with shady palapas and wooden fishing boats. Today, the water beckons. Snorkeling, then lunch at one of the shady rustic beachside restaurants – creamy Oaxacan Queso Fundido (cheese au gratin) and spicy-lime cocktail de pulpo (octopus).

DAY 12 *Transit Panama Canal*

Today we're saving 7,872 miles. Maybe another croissant isn't out of order. One hundred years ago, the ship would have labored around South America. Instead, a continent shortcut and ship-elevator take us from the Pacific to Atlantic Oceans in 10 hours.

The zigzag passage is Zen-slow. Time to reflect upon the jungle greenery all around, the engineering of the enormous gates, the methodical precision of the ship-pulling "mules" (trains), and the bigger-than-anything canal-building quantities of people, rock, mosquitoes and human perspiration. At Isla Tigre, a right zag puts the ship on approach for the final rite of passage, the Gatun Locks. Elevator down, 85 feet. Then past Colon, its twin breakwaters and into the Caribbean Sea. It's water green-blue and aquamarine.

DAY 15 *Port of call, Curacao*

The doll house 17th century Dutch architecture belies the mixed-bag culture that inhabits them – West Indian, Latin American, Jewish and African. They speak Papiamento and listen to reggae, soca and tambu music. They dine on local Karko (conch), Kabritu (goat), keshi yena (cheese filled with chicken, raisins, beans and more) and sometimes, iguana soup.

CHEF'S DINNER

APPETIZERS

Seared Tenderloin of Beef Carpaccio
Fried Caper Parsley Oil

Tian of Premium Seafood and Gin-Cured Salmon
Caviar and Papaya Seed Dressing

Seafood Potpourri in a Saffron Nage
Garlic Crostini

ENTRÉES

Linguine al Pesto alla Moda Ligure
Green Beans, Red Bliss Potatoes and Pine Nuts

Seared Ahi Tuna
Braised Lentils and Saffron Foam

Breast of Chicken à la Kiev
Herb Butter and Baby Vegetables

Rack of Lamb Dijonnaise
Brussels Sprouts, Roasted Garlic Mashed Potatoes and Red Pepper Jus

DESSERTS

Napoleon
Vanilla-Anise Pastry Cream and Blueberry-Tamarillo Sauce

Black Forest Gâteau
Black Cherries, Kirschwasser and Fresh Cream

SEARED TENDERLOIN OF BEEF CARPACCIO

Fried Caper Parsley Oil

Serves 6

1, 1½ to 2-pound trimmed beef tenderloin

1 tablespoon olive oil

3 garlic cloves, chopped

2 teaspoons fresh parsley, chopped

1 teaspoon fresh thyme, chopped

½ teaspoon fresh sage, chopped

½ teaspoon fresh oregano, chopped

salt and pepper

PARSLEY OIL

½ cup extra virgin olive oil

juice from 1 lemon

¼ cup fresh parsley, chopped

salt and pepper

1½ cups large Spanish capers

vegetable oil for frying

1 head curly endive

⅔ cup shaved Parmesan cheese

fresh chives

The pungent, salty flavor of the capers lends itself very well to the mild beef tenderloin. Frying them adds a slight crispness to the otherwise soft-textured dish. Fried capers are also great as an accompaniment to salmon and other fish or even as a snack on their own. The capers will continue to brown a bit once removed from the oil, so be careful not to allow them to become too dark before removing.

Heat a large heavy sauté pan with very little oil over high heat. Rub the tenderloin with olive oil, season generously and coat evenly with the chopped garlic and herbs. Sear the tenderloin in the sauté pan for a few seconds on each side just to brown well, but not to cook the meat.

Wrap the tenderloin tightly with plastic wrap and place in the freezer for 1 to 2 hours just to firm up the meat to facilitate slicing; do not freeze.

Mix the ingredients together for the parsley oil, adjust the seasoning and hold at room temperature.

Heat about 2 cups of vegetable oil in a saucepan for frying. Drain the capers well and fry them all at once in the hot oil. Be careful, the capers will splatter oil out of the pan. Fry the capers until all of their moisture has evaporated and they become brown and crisp. Drain them onto absorbent paper towels. The capers will be salty. If less salt is desired, rinse the capers with fresh water before frying.

Wash and separate the endive. Just before serving, slice the tenderloin very thin, preferably on a slicer. Arrange the slices around the plate and place the endive in the center. Garnish with shaved cheese, chives, parsley oil and fried capers.

PAPAYA

TIAN OF PREMIUM SEAFOOD AND GIN-CURED SALMON

Caviar and Papaya Seed Dressing

Serves 6

1, 1½ to 2-pound side fresh salmon

2 cups fresh dill, rough chopped

zest and juice from 1 orange

zest and juice from 2 limes

zest and juice from 2 lemons

1 cup brown sugar

½ cup salt

2 tablespoons crushed juniper berries

¼ cup gin

SEAFOOD SALAD

½ cup scallops

1 cup shrimp

1 cup crabmeat

½ cup mussel meat

½ cup cucumber, diced

⅔ cup papaya, diced

3 tablespoons fresh chives, chopped

juice from 1 lemon

1¼ cups plain yogurt

salt and pepper

DRESSING

1 cup papaya pulp

½ cup olive oil

¼ cup papaya seeds

¼ cup white wine vinegar

salt and pepper

lemon segments and fresh dill

1, 6-ounce jar salmon caviar

The peppery and slightly bitter papaya seeds make a pleasant, surprising addition to this recipe. Ground, they are an interesting ingredient to add to dressings, sauces, ice creams and even muffins or quick breads. They can also be dried or fried and used as a crispy, crunchy garnish, although they are better eaten in combination with other ingredients.

Lay the salmon side flat, skin-side down, in a large dish. Mix together the chopped dill and all of the zests and spread generously over the filet. Mix the salt, brown sugar and juniper together and spread evenly over the dill and zests. Sprinkle on the juices and gin evenly. Wrap tightly and refrigerate for 36 to 48 hours to allow the salmon to cure.

Prepare the salad by steaming the scallops, shrimp, crab and mussels. The seafood can also be poached in a court-bouillon (p.10) or sautéed. Chill the cooked seafood and cut into small chunks. Mix all of the salad ingredients together and adjust the seasoning. Chill.

Place all of the dressing ingredients into a blender and puree. Adjust the seasoning. Water can be added by the teaspoonful if the dressing is too thick.

To assemble, rinse the marinade off of the salmon side and pat dry. Thinly slice the salmon. The slices can be used as they are, or they can be cut into circles with a pastry cutter. Lay a piece of salmon on the plate. Top it with a generous portion of the seafood salad and a second piece of salmon. This can all be done in a pastry ring for presentation.

Drizzle the dressing around casually and garnish with lemon segments, fresh dill and salmon caviar.

SEAFOOD POTPOURRI IN A SAFFRON NAGE

Garlic Crostini

Serves 6

12 small clams

12 black mussels

12 large prawns

24 bay scallops

CROSTINI

2 tablespoons olive oil

4 garlic cloves, chopped

1 loaf thick crust baguette

salt and pepper

NAGE

20 threads saffron

juice from 2 lemons

6 cups fish stock (p. 220)

1/4 cup carrot, julienne

1/4 cup zucchini, julienne

1/4 cup red pepper, julienne

1/4 cup leek, julienne

1 tablespoon butter

1/2 cup fresh cream

salt and pepper

fresh herbs

Saffron, the world's most expensive spice, comes from the small crocus flower. It takes approximately 15,000 flowers to produce 1 ounce of saffron. Saffron is sold in threads or powder. Threads are preferred as the powder is often diluted with imitations. The threads should be steeped or placed into cold liquid before use. Placing the threads into hot liquid seals the outsides and makes it difficult to extract the rich color and flavor. Saffron is a wonderful addition to rice, pastas, soups and some pastries.

Preheat oven to 400°F. Slice the baguette thinly on an angle. Brush the slices on both sides with olive oil; rub on the chopped garlic and season with the salt and pepper. Place on a baking tray and bake until crisp and brown on both sides, turning them at least once.

Put the saffron threads and lemon juice in the cold fish stock, bring to a boil together and then reduce to a simmer. Poach the seafood in the fish stock. The clams and mussels will take approximately 7 minutes, the prawns 5 minutes and the scallops 3 to 4 minutes. Add the julienne vegetables and cook for 1 minute longer. Reduce the heat to low and swirl in the fresh cream and the butter. Adjust the seasoning. The broth will be thin.

Serve in a soup plate, arranging the seafood and vegetables nicely and pouring the saffron nage over it. Garnish with the crostini and fresh herbs.

PESTO

LINGUINE AL PESTO ALLA MODA LIGURE

Green Beans, Red Bliss Potatoes and Pine Nuts

Serves 6

1 pound red bliss potatoes

½ pound fresh green beans

1½ pounds dried linguine

BASIL PESTO

3 cups fresh basil leaves

4 large garlic cloves

½ cup pine nuts

1½ cups extra virgin olive oil

1¼ cups Parmesan cheese, grated

salt and pepper

fresh basil

½ cup pine nuts

The secrets to an excellent pesto are to begin with the finest ingredients, to not over-mix or pound the basil, and to prepare it as fresh as possible just before serving. A fresh sweet basil, good quality extra virgin olive oil and real Parmigiano-Reggiano cheese are ideal. If you have left-over pesto, place it in an airtight container with enough olive oil in it to cover completely and refrigerate for 1 or 2 days. Keeping the pesto for a longer period or freezing it will negatively affect its flavor.

In a blender, puree the basil, garlic, pine nuts and olive oil until a smooth paste is formed. Do not over blend or the mixture will get hot and darken. Transfer to a bowl, mix in the Parmesan cheese and season with the salt and pepper.

Place the red bliss potatoes in 2 quarts of cold, salted water and bring to a boil. Continue to boil until the potatoes are tender, but not falling apart. Remove from the water, slice and season with salt and pepper.

Meanwhile, blanch the green beans in 2 quarts of salted boiling water for approximately 6 minutes or until just tender, but still crisp. If the beans will not be served immediately, chill them in ice water to prevent them from over cooking and turning brown.

Bring 6 quarts of salted water to a boil. Boil the pasta until al dente, approximately 8 minutes.

In a large sauté pan, combine the cooked pasta, potato slices, green beans and a generous amount of pesto to coat well. Heat it all together thoroughly and adjust the seasoning.

Preheat oven to 400°F. Toast the pine nuts for garnishing by placing them in the oven and cooking until light brown, turning often. The pine nuts will continue to darken slightly once removed from the oven.

Serve the pasta with the potatoes and beans in a large bowl or plate. Garnish with toasted whole pine nuts, fresh basil and grated Parmesan cheese.

SEARED AHI TUNA

Braised Lentils and Saffron Foam

Serves 6

6, 6 to 7-ounce ahi tuna filets, sashimi grade

salt and pepper

3 tablespoons olive oil

BRAISED LENTILS

1 1/2 cups brown lentils

2 teaspoons butter

1/4 cup onion, chopped

1 teaspoon garlic, chopped

1/4 cup carrot, small dice

1/4 cup celery, small dice

2 tablespoons balsamic vinegar

3 cups water, chicken or vegetable stock (p. 221)

1/2 cup demi-glace (p. 220)

2 teaspoons fresh thyme, chopped

salt and pepper

SAFFRON FOAM

10 threads saffron

1/4 cup vermouth

2 small shallots, chopped

5 white peppercorns

1 sprig fresh thyme

1 cup dry white wine

1 cup fresh cream

3 tablespoons butter

salt and pepper

2 medium zucchini

fresh thyme

A sashimi grade Ahi tuna should be used for this preparation. The tuna should be dark red and firm. It should be served rare to medium rare as longer cooking will make it tough and dry.

Wash the lentils well and sort to remove any foreign objects. Soak the lentils in water until soft. This only takes a few hours, but can be done overnight in the refrigerator.

Melt the butter in a saucepan. Sauté the onions until soft, add the garlic and sauté 2 minutes more. Add the carrots and celery and sauté until they just begin to soften. Drain the soaked lentils and add, sautéing for 4 minutes. Add the balsamic vinegar and reduce until almost dry. Add the water or stock and simmer until the lentils are soft. The mixture should be wet, but not soupy at this stage. Add the demi-glace and the fresh thyme and simmer until the liquid has formed a rich sauce. Adjust the seasoning.

For the saffron foam, place the saffron threads in the vermouth and steep for about 10 minutes or until the saffron color begins to bleed into the vermouth. Add the shallots, peppercorns, thyme, white wine and vermouth with the saffron to a saucepan. Simmer the liquid and reduce to a syrup. The mixture should be a dark orange color, but be careful not to burn. Remove the reduction from the heat and cool slightly. Meanwhile, whip the cream to a soft peak. Whisk the cold butter into the reduction over a very low heat. Strain the reduction and butter mixture into the whipped cream and combine well. Adjust the seasoning and keep in a warm place, but do not heat over a direct source.

Using a parisienne scoop (melon baller), scoop out at least 18 balls of zucchini. Steam or blanch the zucchini in salted boiling water until just soft, but still crisp, 3 to 4 minutes. Toss with butter and season.

Just before serving, heat the olive oil in a large heavy sauté pan over high heat. Season the ahi tuna filets generously with salt and pepper. Sear the tuna filets for approximately 30 seconds on all sides for rare tuna. Be careful not to over cook the tuna or it will become dry and tough.

Arrange the tuna in slices over a bed of the braised lentils. Drizzle the saffron sauce around and serve with the parisienne zucchini and fresh thyme leaves.

BREAST OF CHICKEN À LA KIEV

Herb Butter and Baby Vegetables

Serves 6

6 half, large airline chicken breasts, skinned

seasoned flour for dusting

1 egg, beaten

1 to 1½ cups bread crumbs

HERB BUTTER

1½ cups butter

1 teaspoon tarragon, chopped

1 teaspoon chives, chopped

1 teaspoon parsley, chopped

1 teaspoon garlic, minced

1 teaspoon mustard

dash Worcestershire sauce

dash Tabasco sauce

salt and pepper

6 baby beets

12 baby turnips

vegetable oil for frying

Herb butter is an easy way to add a lot of flavor to a meat, seafood or vegetable dish. The butter can be mixed with any combination of herbs that you like along with spices, mustards, wine or other flavorings. The butter can be prepared well in advance which makes for easy use and allows for the flavors to combine. If you make the butter in large batches, you can then wrap it well in smaller portions and freeze it up to 3 months.

Mix all herb butter ingredients together well and chill.

Pound out the chicken breast with a meat mallet to a ¼-inch thick. The wing bone can be trimmed and left on for garnish, or cut off. Season the breast meat. Divide the herb butter into six portions and roll into finger-shaped cylinders. Place one cylinder in the center of each breast. Roll the breast up around the herb butter.

Preheat the oil to 360°F. Dust the stuffed chicken breasts with the seasoned flour. Dip each breast in the beaten egg and then coat well with the breadcrumbs. Fry the chicken breasts in the oil until golden brown and cooked through.

Meanwhile, trim the tops of the turnips and beets. Peel the turnips, but not the beets. In a small pan, place the baby beets in 3 cups of cold water and bring to a boil. Cook for approximately 8 minutes or until tender, strain. The easiest way to peel the beets is by using a kitchen towel or heavy duty paper towel and gently rubbing the beets in the towel. The peel should come off easily. The baby turnips need to be cooked separately using the same method. When the vegetables are cooked, split them in halves; toss them in butter and season.

Serve the chicken breast with the vegetables. The melted herb butter will run out once the breast is cut.

RACK OF LAMB DIJONNAISE

Brussels Sprouts, Roasted Garlic Mashed Potatoes and Red Pepper Jus

Serves 6

4 lamb racks, frenched

oil for searing

Dijon mustard for coating

1 cup bread crumbs

½ teaspoon rosemary, chopped

1 teaspoon thyme, chopped

3 tablespoons melted butter

salt and pepper

RED PEPPER JUS

8 whole red bell peppers

2 teaspoons oil

1 clove garlic

½ teaspoon mustard

1 cup lamb jus or demi-glace (p. 219)

½ teaspoon thyme, chopped

salt and pepper

MASHED POTATOES

2 pounds red bliss potatoes

1 bulb garlic

½ cup milk

¼ cup butter

salt and pepper

1 pound Brussels sprouts

1 teaspoon butter

1 teaspoon sugar

salt and pepper

fresh rosemary

Preheat oven to 375°F. Season the lamb racks and sear well on all sides in a hot pan with a little oil. Once seared, remove and coat the top (fat side) generously with Dijon mustard. Mix bread crumb ingredients together and coat each rack with the bread crumbs, pressing firmly so that the crumbs stay together and stick to the mustard and rack.

Place the lamb in the hot oven for approximately 15 minutes for medium. When the lamb is cooked, remove it from the oven and let it rest for at least 5 minutes before cutting the chops.

Begin the sauce by roasting the peppers. This can be done well in advance, even the day before. Rub the whole bell peppers with a little oil and place under the broiler or over an open flame such as a grill. The skin should char and bubble on all sides. When the skin is charred, place the peppers in a large bowl and cover tightly with plastic wrap. The steam created by the peppers will help loosen the skin. Once cooled, remove the peppers from the bowl and take off the skin with your fingers or a small knife. Split the peppers and remove the seeds. Cut one pepper into small dices to be served with the Brussels sprouts.

Place the remaining peppers, garlic clove, mustard, lamb jus or demi-glace and thyme in a saucepan. Simmer gently for approximately 20 minutes, removing the foam that comes to the surface. Puree the sauce and strain it. Adjust the seasoning.

Trim the spots off of the red bliss potatoes and remove approximately half of the peel. Put the potatoes in a large pot well covered with cold, salted water and bring to a boil. Boil until just tender.

Meanwhile, place the whole garlic bulb in a hot oven to roast. This can be done together with the lamb. Roast the garlic until tender, remove from oven and squeeze the garlic flesh out of the bulb. Heat the milk, butter and roasted garlic in a pan large enough to hold the potatoes. Drain the cooked potatoes and add them to the milk mixture. Use a potato ricer or a hand mixer to mash the potatoes to a rough texture. Season well.

Trim and halve the Brussels sprouts. Steam them until just tender. Melt the butter and sugar together in a pan, do not caramelize and toss the cooked sprouts with it. Add in the reserved diced red peppers and adjust the seasoning.

Serve the lamb in double chops with the potatoes, sauce and Brussels sprouts. Garnish with fresh rosemary.

NAPOLEON

Vanilla-Anise Pastry Cream, Blueberry-Tamarillo Sauce

Serves 6 to 8

PASTRY CREAM

1 1/2 cups whole milk

1 vanilla bean

1/2 cup sugar

1/4 cup flour

4 egg yolks

1/2 cup fresh cream

teaspoon sugar

anise, ground

3 frozen puff pastry sheets
(sheets can be purchased in the freezer section of your local supermarket and are usually 1-foot x 1-foot square)

TAMARILLO SAUCE

1 pint fresh blueberries

4 tamarillos, peeled

1/8 cup Pernod

1 teaspoon sugar

fondant (p. 218)

2 ounces semi-sweet chocolate

fresh mint leaves

To prepare the pastry cream, bring the milk and vanilla bean just to the boiling point. Meanwhile, mix the sugar, flour and egg yolks together to form a smooth paste. Remove the vanilla bean from the milk and slowly mix the milk into the paste mixture. Return the mixture to the stove over a double boiler. Do not boil again. Scrape the seeds from the vanilla bean and add to the mixture. Continue cooking until it has thickened enough to heavily coat the back of a spoon. Remove from heat and continue to stir until cooled to room temperature.

Whip the fresh cream to a stiff peak and sweeten with the sugar. Fold in the ground anise as desired. Fold 1 cup of the pastry cream into the whipped cream mixture and chill.

Preheat oven to 450°F. Place the sheets of puff pastry on individual lightly buttered baking trays. Use a fork to make several uniform holes in the pastry to prevent it from rising. Bake for approximately 20 to 25 minutes or until golden brown and crisp. Once baked, gently remove from the baking trays and cool.

Add all of the ingredients for the sauce (reserving a few fresh blueberries for garnish) into a saucepan and heat gently together until the mixture has cooked down. Blend the sauce with a hand mixer to smooth out while not breaking the seeds.

Spread the anise pastry cream evenly over one layer of the pastry. Add the second layer and press to distribute the cream evenly. Top the with the remaining pastry cream. Add the third layer of pastry and press again. Refrigerate for approximately 30 minutes.

Meanwhile, heat the fondant and the chocolate separately over double boilers to melt. Place the chocolate in a small piping bag with a fine tip and keep warm. Remove the Napoleon from the refrigerator and pour the warm fondant over the top in one motion and smooth with a spatula. Working quickly, draw lines across the fondant with the chocolate. Use a small knife or a toothpick to drag the fondant across the chocolate lines working back and forth in alternating directions.

Use a serrated bread knife to cut the Napoleon. Serve with the sauce, a few fresh berries and mint leaves.

BLACK FOREST GÂTEAU

Black Cherries, Kirschwasser and Fresh Cream

Makes one 9-inch cake

CHOCOLATE SPONGE

6 egg yolks

1 cup sugar

½ teaspoon vanilla essence

juice from 1 lemon

¼ cup sweet white wine

1 cup flour

⅓ cup cocoa powder

1 teaspoon baking powder

⅛ teaspoon salt

4 egg whites

(Grated lemon or orange zest can be added. The white wine can be replaced with different flavored alcohol.)

2, 15-ounce cans black cherries

SYRUP

1 cup juice from cherries

juice from 1 lemon

½ cup sugar

1 stick cinnamon

¼ cup Kirschwasser

1 quart fresh cream

¼ cup sugar

chocolate shavings

This relatively easy dessert is made great by the combination of rich chocolate, black cherries and sweet fresh cream. The chocolate sponge and the cherry syrup can be prepared a day in advance, wrapped tightly and refrigerated. If this is done, allow both items to come to room temperature before finishing the cake. The gâteau should be prepared as close to serving as possible so that the cream remains fresh and the juice from the cherries does not bleed.

Begin by preparing the chocolate sponge. Preheat oven to 350°F. Whisk the egg yolks and sugar together over a hot water bath until more than doubled in volume. Add the vanilla, lemon juice and wine and whisk. You want to incorporate as much air as possible. Remove from the water bath and cool. Sift the flour, cocoa powder, baking powder and salt together and gently fold into the egg mix. Whisk the egg whites to a stiff peak and gently fold into the mix. Grease and flour the cake pan. Pour the mixture in to fill the pan ⅔ full. Bake for 40 minutes or until a toothpick inserted into the center comes out clean. The sponge should not become too brown, nor dry out. Once baked, cool the sponge on a wire rack. Wrap tightly with plastic wrap if refrigerating. Split into three layers using a serrated knife.

Mix the ingredients for the syrup together and heat to dissolve, remove the cinnamon stick and chill.

Whip the cream and sugar to a medium-stiff peak.

Begin assembling the cake. Place one layer of the chocolate sponge on a cake stand and sprinkle generously with the cherry syrup. Spread a ½-inch layer of the cream and push half of the cherries into the cream. Top with the second cake layer and repeat the process. Top with the third layer of cake. Sprinkle with syrup and decorate the top and sides with the remainder of the cream. Garnish generously with chocolate shavings and more cherries.

EUROPE

Journal – Europe

DAY 3 *Port of call, Bilbao, Spain*

Frank Gehry meets the Basques. Progressive contemporary art and old, deep-rooted culture. With great rustic-rooted food. In this 700-hundred year old city on the Bay of Bizcaya, everyone – tourists and residents – appreciates the wavy sheets of stainless steel rising up into the small angular mountain that is Gehry's designed Guggenheim Museum.

In the cozy neighborhood of Casco Viejo, a "poteo" and "tapeo" crawl commences, going from restaurant to bar tasting "tapas" (savory snacks) and "potes" (little glasses of fruity Spanish wine). Come to think of it, this highly sociable mix of culinary treats and happy company is rather like life on the ship.

Port of call, Bordeaux, France (Le Verdon)

For wine lovers, docking the ship on the La Garonne river near Bordeaux must be the equivalent of opera lovers sitting in the front row at the Met. There are narrow-streeted neighborhoods, gardens, open-air markets and Gothic cathedrals to visit – we opt for a gastronomic excursion to one of the chateaux in the Pauillac region. Lunch is mouclade (mussel stew made with wine and shallots) and tournedos of beef with Bordelaise sauce (the great wine reduction sauce was invented here), and, of course, a glass or two of...

Port of call, Glasgow, Scotland (Greenock)

If ships have souls – and they do – then ours must be bowing with respect as she steams up the Firth of Clyde, nearing the birthplace of many legendary vessels. The ship turns with the river past the Scottish brown-green hills (always a surprise to golf enthusiasts used to the uniform green of watered-lawns) and puts in at Greenock.

FRENCH DINNER

APPETIZERS

Escargots à la Bourguignonne
Brioche, Café de Paris Butter and Tomato Compote

Soupe à l'Oignon Gratinée
Caramelized Onion, Sherry and Gruyère Cheese

ENTRÉES

Nouilles Façon Cannebière
Egg Fettuccine Simmered in a Light Creamy Lobster Sauce

Grenouilles Provençal
Gently Sautéed Frog Legs, White Wine and Polenta

Canard à l'Orange
Roasted Duckling Glazed with Orange Sauce, Williams Potato

Porc Normande
Pork Loin Calvados Flambé, Baked Apple and Glazed Carrots

DESSERTS

Raspberry Crème Brûlée
Amber Caramel

Tarte Tatin
Caramelized Apple, Puff Pastry and Buttermilk Ice Cream

There's much talk of seeking out haggis (basically sheep innards, mixed and baked with beef suet and lightly toasted oatmeal), but we decide on a tour of the Charles Rennie Mackintosh designed Scotland Street School, one of the many monuments of early craftsman architecture (before it was imported to the U.S.). And, we get to taste a Black Bun, a dark colored fruit cake made with raisins, currants, finely-chopped peel, chopped almonds and brown sugar.

DAY 8 *Port of call, Cork, Ireland*

The Irish Sea, often like the celebrated rough and tumble Irishman well into an evening of Guinness-drinking, is remarkably well-behaved on the way down from Scotland to Ireland's bottom coast where the sparkling green Cork awaits us.

A half-day excursion challenges our speaking abilities as the names of the several towns and villages roll off our tongues, names such as Innishannon, Ballinascarthy, Clonakilty, Rosscarbery and Skibberbeen (stopping at the Jameson's distillery is particularly helpful in the expansion of one's local vocabulary, or at least it seems that way at the time).

DAY 9 *Port of call, Devon/Cornwall, England (Plymouth)*

We fly past the Isles of Scylla, Land's End, Penzance (as in Gilbert and Sullivan's pirates), Lizard Point, Gribbin Head, Rame Head (there's a scary movie in these names) and into the great bay of Plymouth.

DAY 11 *Port of call, Amsterdam, The Netherlands*

The ship comes in from the North Sea through a series of locks to the new whale-like passenger terminal. It is walking distance to the city center – off we go to see the Golden Age Canals with the old, gabled canal houses and vividly-painted houseboats.

Lunch of erwtensoep (thick pea soup with sausage) and then out to the Van Gogh museum – more of his paintings here than anywhere else in the world. There's even time for a stop at the Heinneken Brewery.

DAY 12 *Port of call, Brussels/Bruges, Belgium (Zeebrugge)*

We wander, our last full day on the cruise, through the ancient neighborhoods, past the antique houses of 16 century painters, thinking about the course of history, wondering what people 2000 years from now will say about our culture and our global travels. Hopefully, they'll be able to pronounce our names.

ACROSS THE FLEET, WE SERVE MORE THAN 75,000 MEALS A DAY.

ESCARGOTS À LA BOURGUIGNONNE

Brioche, Café de Paris Butter and Tomato Compote

Serves 6

brioche (p. 217)

36 escargots, cleaned, fresh or canned

1 medium carrot, rough chopped

1 small onion, rough chopped

1 celery stalk, rough chopped

1 bay leaf

6 black peppercorns

fresh thyme

1 quart court-bouillon (p. 10)

salt

CAFÉ DE PARIS BUTTER

3/4 cup butter

1 tablespoon shallots, minced

1 clove garlic, minced

1 tablespoon parsley, chopped

1 teaspoon mustard

1 egg yolk

1 dash Worcestershire sauce

1/4 cup burgundy wine

salt and pepper

TOMATO COMPOTE

1 1/2 cups tomato, small dice, peeled and seeded

2 cloves garlic, minced

1/4 cup balsamic vinegar

2 tablespoons extra virgin olive oil

2 teaspoons fresh thyme, chopped

salt and pepper

Snails are considered one of, if not the first animal eaten by man. They can be purchased fresh, but are usually sold canned. Fresh snails should be soaked in a brine solution, cleaned and poached the same day of purchase before any further preparation. The French native petit-gris species is now raised in America and is the most commonly consumed. Although very popular and delicious, French culinary writer Nicolas de Bonefons wrote once that he was "astonished that the odd tastes of man have led him as far as this depraved dish in order to satisfy the extravagance of gluttony."

Prepare the brioche.

Preheat oven to 425°F. Slice the brioche into 1-inch thick slices. Use a cutter to cut out 2-inch round disks from the slices and pinch a small amount of bread out of the center of the disk to form a well. Place the disks on a baking tray in oven and toast to a light brown.

Meanwhile, drain the escargots if using canned. Add the escargots, vegetables, herbs and court-bouillon to a pan and bring to a simmer. Cook until the escargots are tender, approximately 10 minutes for canned or 25 minutes for fresh.

Prepare the Café de Paris butter by creaming all of the ingredients together and chill. Mix all of the ingredients for the tomato compote together and let marinate.

Preheat the broiler. Place the brioche disks on a baking tray. Place 1 escargot on each disk. Top generously with the butter. Place under the broiler for 1 to 2 minutes until the butter has browned.

Serve with the tomato compote and fresh thyme leaves.

SOUPE À L'OIGNION GRATINÉE

Caramelized Onion, Sherry and Gruyère Cheese

Serves 6

3 tablespoons butter

4 cups onion, sliced

6 cups beef stock (p. 220)

1 cup demi-glace (p. 220)
(The demi-glace can be replaced with more beef stock. Chicken stock or water can also be used for all of the liquid, but the soup will be far less rich.)

1 bay leaf

6 black peppercorns

2 teaspoons fresh thyme, chopped

1/4 cup dry sherry

salt and pepper

6 slices bread, trimmed and toasted

1 1/2 cups Gruyère cheese, shredded

parsley, chopped

Although made popular by the French, a Spanish sweet yellow onion is the best for this recipe. The key to well caramelized onions is patience. Cook the onions slowly, stirring occasionally and allow them to become dark and rich in color and aroma. This recipe lends itself well to variations by using different cheeses such as a Munster, Saint-Paulin or even Roquefort along with various fortified wines or bourbons.

Melt the butter in a heavy stock pot and sauté the onions slowly until well caramelized to a rich brown. Add the remaining ingredients for the soup except the sherry. Cook together for at least 30 minutes until the flavors are well developed. Adjust the seasoning and add the sherry.

Preheat oven to 400°F. Pour the soup into oven-proof soup cups. Top each cup with a slice of the toasted bread and then the shredded cheese. Place the soup cups on a baking tray and bake until the cheese has melted and browned slightly. Sprinkle with chopped parsley and serve.

NOUILLES FAÇON CANNEBIÈRE

Egg Fettuccine Simmered in a Light Creamy Lobster Sauce

Serves 6

3 rock lobster tails

1 quart court-bouillon (p. 10)

1½ pounds dried fettuccine noodles

3 tablespoons olive oil

2 tablespoons shallots, minced

1 clove garlic, minced

1 cup court-bouillon, reserved from cooking the lobster

½ cup fresh cream

3 cups cooked rich tomato sauce (p. 217)

¼ cup cognac

1 tablespoon fresh tarragon leaves

salt and pepper

Pasta is made primarily from water and semolina flour ground out of durum wheat. Additional ingredients include olive oil, eggs, salt, natural colorings and flavorings. Pasta made with eggs is considered superior. The dough can be shaped into hundreds of varieties and is sold fresh, dried and frozen. All pasta should be cooked in large amounts of salted water until just tender and firm to the bite, "al dente."

Bring the court-bouillon to a boil and poach the lobster tails for approximately 8 minutes. Remove the lobster tails and run under cold water to cool. Strain 1 cup of the court-bouillon for the sauce.

Remove the lobster meat from the shell and break or cut into large chunks.

Bring at least 6 quarts of salted water to a boil. Add the pasta and stir gently to prevent the pasta from sticking together. Boil the pasta until al dente. Strain.

While the pasta is being boiled, heat the olive oil in a large sauté pan and sauté the shallots, garlic and lobster together. Add the court-bouillon and reduce by half. Add the cream and reduce again. Add the cognac and cook for 3 minutes. Add the tomato sauce and the tarragon and adjust the seasoning.

Toss the pasta and sauce together and serve in large bowls with plenty of fresh tarragon.

GRENOUILLES PROVENÇAL

Gently Sautéed Frog Legs, White Wine and Polenta

Serves 6

fresh tomato sauce (p. 114)

2 tablespoons olive oil

½ cup onion, small diced

12 garlic cloves

¼ cup black olives, pitted and sliced

2 tablespoons capers

¼ cup white wine

3 teaspoons fresh oregano

salt and pepper

18 pairs frog legs

2 cups milk

2 bay leaves

6 white peppercorns, crushed

olive oil

flour for dusting

salt and pepper

POLENTA

4 cups chicken stock (p. 221)

1½ cups yellow cornmeal

3 tablespoons butter

¼ cup Parmesan cheese, grated

salt and pepper

fresh oregano

Legs, the only edible part of the frog, are delicate in flavor and aroma. The meat toughens as it cooks which means they should be prepared either by short cooking methods such as a sauté or by stewing for a longer period of time until the meat has become tender again. Although frog legs are gaining in popularity, the United States exports many more frog legs than it consumes. They are a good alternative to fish or seafood and are often eaten during Lent.

Place the cleaned frog legs into a shallow dish. Pour the milk over. Add the bay leaves and crushed white pepper. Marinate in the refrigerator for two hours.

Prepare the fresh tomato sauce. In a separate pan heat the olive oil and sauté the onions until tender. Increase the heat; add the garlic cloves and brown. Add the olives and capers and cook for 3 minutes. Add white wine and reduce. Add the tomato sauce and gently simmer for 10 minutes. Add the oregano and adjust the seasoning.

Meanwhile, bring the chicken stock to a boil. Whisk in the cornmeal and reduce the heat to simmer. Cook for approximately 20 minutes, stirring regularly to prevent burning. Just before serving, stir in the butter and the Parmesan cheese and season well.

Heat enough olive oil in a sauté pan to shallow fry the frog legs. Remove the legs from the milk. Season with salt and pepper and dust with flour. Sauté gently until golden brown and tender, approximately 6 minutes. Remove from the oil and lightly season again.

To serve, spoon the polenta in the center of the plate and stand the frog legs up around the polenta. Generously spoon the Provençal sauce around the plate and garnish with more fresh oregano.

CANARD À L'ORANGE

Roasted Duckling Glazed with Orange Sauce, Williams Potato

Serves 6

3, 4-pound ducklings

1 green apple

1 orange

1 onion

2 carrots

2 celery stalks

fresh thyme

salt and pepper

slices from 1 orange

duchesse potatoes (p. 171)

flour for dusting

2 eggs

1 cup bread crumbs

vegetable oil for frying

salt and pepper

SAUCE

½ cup white wine

¼ cup brandy

1½ cups chicken stock (p. 221)

1 cup orange juice

½ cup demi-glace (p. 220)

salt and pepper

½ pound yellow French beans

½ pound green French beans

salt and pepper

leek strips

The classical Pommes de Terre Williams gets its name from being shaped like a Williams pear. The shape is quite easy to achieve and makes for an interesting presentation and conversation piece. They can be shaped and breaded in advance and fried at the last minute. Use a small fresh herb or a piece of dried pasta to represent the stem of the pear. A clove is sometimes used in the bottom for garnish, but warn your guests not to bite into it.

Preheat the oven to 450°F. Wash the ducklings and trim off any excess fat. Season the cavities well with salt, pepper and thyme. Rough cut the apple, orange, onion, carrots and celery, including peels and mix. Stuff the cavities and place ducklings in a roasting pan.

Heat in the oven for 15 minutes, then reduce the temperature to 350°F and roast for approximately 1½ hours longer until the duck is cooked through. Place the orange slices in with the duck for the last 20 minutes to caramelize and use as garnish.

While the ducks are roasting, prepare the duchesse potatoes. Let cool enough to be handled and form the potatoes into small pear shapes. Dip the potato pears in flour, then egg and finally in the bread crumbs. Heat a small pan of oil or deep fryer and fry the potatoes just before serving to a golden brown. Drain on a paper towel and lightly season.

Remove the ducks from the oven and pour off any excess fat from the roasting pan. Add the stuffing from the cavities back into the roasting pan and keep the ducks warm. Place the roasting pan on a burner on moderate heat. Add the white wine and brandy to the roasting pan and reduce, scraping all of the particles from the bottom of the pan. Add the stock, orange juice and demi-glace and reduce by half to thicken. Strain the sauce and season.

Bring 2 quarts of salted water to a boil. Boil the trimmed beans until just tender, but still crisp. Remove from the water and season. The beans can be wrapped up in bundles by quickly boiling whole chives or strips of leeks to wrap around the beans.

Carve the duck as desired and serve with the beans, potatoes, sauce and caramelized oranges.

PORC NORMANDE

Pork Loin Calvados Flambé, Baked Apple and Glazed Carrots

Serves 6

1, 7-rib pork loin roast

salt and pepper

3 tablespoons sage, chopped

8 crabapples

ALMOND MACAIRE POTATOES

duchesse potatoes (p. 171)

flour for dusting

2 eggs

1 cup almond slivers

salt and pepper

vegetable oil for frying

SAUCE

½ cup white wine

½ cup Calvados (apple brandy)

1½ cups apple juice

1 cup veal stock (p. 221)

½ cup demi-glace (p. 220)

salt and pepper

GLAZED CARROTS

18 to 24 baby carrots, peeled

½ cup apple juice

½ cup water

½ teaspoon mustard

1 teaspoon honey

2 teaspoons brown sugar

1 teaspoon butter

¼ cup chopped walnuts

salt and pepper

Calvados is an apple brandy made in Calvados, France. It is great for cooking as its dry characteristics leave behind a clean aftertaste of ripe apples and aged oak. Calvados compliments all white meats and makes a great pairing when cooked fruits are served together with savory dishes. Calvados is also a popular variation in desserts for sauces, spice cakes, pies and puddings.

Preheat the oven to 450°F. Rub the pork loin with salt, pepper and sage. In a roasting pan, place the pork loin in the oven. After 15 minutes, reduce the temperature to 325°F and roast for approximately 1½ hours longer until the pork is cooked through. The internal temperature should be 165°F. Halve the crabapples and place in the roasting pan for the last 20 minutes.

While the pork is roasting, prepare the duchesse potatoes. Let cool enough to be handled and form the potatoes into small balls. Dip the potato balls in flour, then egg and finally in the almond slivers. Heat a small pan of oil or deep fryer and fry the potatoes just before serving to a golden brown. Drain on a paper towel and lightly season.

Remove the pork from the oven and pour off any excess fat from the roasting pan. Place the pork loin somewhere to keep warm. Put the roasting pan on a burner on moderate heat. Add the white wine and Calvados to the roasting pan and reduce, scraping all of the particles from the bottom of the pan. Add the stock, apple juice and demi-glace and reduce by half to thicken. Strain the sauce and season.

Place all ingredients for the carrots in a saucepan. Cover and simmer for 12 minutes until the carrots are just tender. Remove the lid and allow the liquid to reduce and slightly caramelize. Adjust the seasoning.

Carve the pork loin as desired and serve with the crabapple, carrots, Macaire potatoes and sauce.

RASPBERRY CRÈME BRÛLÉE

Amber Caramel

Serves 6

CUSTARD

2 cups fresh cream

1 vanilla bean

5 egg yolks

¼ cup sugar

1 cup red raspberries

1 cup golden raspberries

CARAMEL

1 cup sugar

¼ cup water

1 dash of fresh lemon juice

fresh mint leaves

Caramel is a very easy way to make unique garnishes for your desserts that are sure to impress your family and guests. A little practice is all it takes to get the technique down; use your imagination and different items around the kitchen to create different shapes. Work with the caramel only when you have time to be free of interruptions and be careful not to burn yourself with the hot sugar.

To prepare the custard, bring the cream and vanilla bean just to the boiling point. Meanwhile, mix the sugar and egg yolks together to form a smooth paste. Remove the vanilla bean from the milk and slowly mix the milk into the eggs and sugar mixture. Return to the stove over a double boiler; do not boil. Scrape the seeds from the vanilla bean and add to the mixture. Continue cooking for 2 to 3 minutes until it has slightly thickened. Remove from the heat and fold in the raspberries, reserving a few to garnish each plate.

Preheat the oven to 325°F. Place 6, 5-ounce custard cups or molds in a water bath by placing them in a baking pan and pouring enough water in the pan to cover half way up the sides of the molds, being careful to keep the inside of the molds dry. Equally divide the custard in to the molds and bake for 20 to 25 minutes or until the custard has set.

The crème brûlée can be served hot or cold. If you want to remove the custard from the mold for presentation purposes, chill well first.

For the caramel, combine all ingredients in a heavy saucepan, preferably copper. Bring the mixture to a simmer slowly over a moderate heat. Stir the mixture occasionally, but only until it is about to boil. Do not stir after this point or the mixture may crystallize. Use a pastry brush dipped in fresh water to wipe any sugar crystals from the inner sides of the pan while the sugar is cooking. The caramel should be removed from the heat when it has reached 320°F to 340°F. The sugar will continue to darken slightly upon standing. The sugar can be cooked longer if a dark caramel is preferred. Place a piece of parchment paper on a smooth surface or lightly oil a marble or granite surface. Using a fork dipped in the caramel, drizzle the caramel back and forth onto the paper forming a large web like pattern. Use a large, slightly oiled knife to cut the caramel into uniform pieces, or simply break it into free flowing shapes by hand.

Place the custard in the center of a plate and garnish with the caramel lattice, raspberries and mint leaf.

3,800 FOOD AND BEVERAGE PROFESSIONALS REPRESENTING 28 NATIONALITIES...

THAT'S A LOT OF PEOPLE PROVIDING EXCELLENT SERVICE!

TARTE TATIN

Caramelized Apple, Puff Pastry and Buttermilk Ice Cream

Serves 6

ICE CREAM
1½ cups heavy cream

1 cup buttermilk

1 each vanilla bean

7 tablespoons sugar

5 egg yolks

APPLE CHIPS
2 red Fuji apples

1 cup water

juice from a lemon

CARAMEL APPLE SAUCE
½ cup sugar

¼ cup water

¼ cup apple cider

TART
6 Granny Smith apples

2 tablespoons sugar

½ teaspoon cinnamon

2 tablespoons brandy

6 flakes butter

2 frozen puff pastry sheets
(sheets can be purchased in the freezer section of your local supermarket and are usually 1-foot x 1-foot square)

fresh basil buds

Originally a means of preservation, drying fruits and vegetables has become a fashionable way to introduce variety in shape, flavor and texture to desserts and salads. Just about any fruit or vegetable can be dried into a fanciful chip using a low temperature oven or dehydrator.

To prepare the ice cream, bring the cream, milk and vanilla bean just to the boiling point. Meanwhile, mix the sugar and egg yolks together to form a smooth paste. Remove the vanilla bean and slowly mix the milk into the paste mixture. Return to the stove over a double boiler; do not boil. Scrape the seeds from the vanilla bean and add to the mixture. Continue cooking until it has thickened enough to heavily coat the back of a spoon. Remove from heat and strain through a fine sieve and stir over a water bath until chilled. Freeze in an ice cream machine.

To prepare the apple chips, slice the whole apples vertically, removing only the seeds from the slices. Mix the water and lemon juice together and dip each for a few seconds to prevent the apples from turning brown. Place the apple slices on a parchment paper lined baking tray and put in the oven. Set the oven on 150°F. The apples will take from 30 minutes to 2 hours to dry.

Prepare the sauce by cooking the sugar and water together for 5 minutes or just until the sugar starts to brown. Add the apple cider and cook 4 minutes more. The sauce will thicken slightly as it cools.

Peel and core the apples. Cut the apples in half and thinly slice. Toss the apple slices together with the sugar, cinnamon and brandy.

Preheat oven to 375°F. Place 6, 5 to 6 inch pie pans on a baking sheet. Pour enough of the caramel apple sauce into the bottom of each pan to just cover it well. Put one flake of butter into each pie pan. Layer the apples into the bottom of each pan in a tight circular fan pattern. Cut the puff pastry into circles the same size as the pie pans and place one circle of pastry over the apples. Bake for 20 minutes or until the pastry has browned and the apples have softened.

Let the apple tarts cool slightly and invert them onto serving plates. Top each with a scoop of ice cream and an apple chip. Drizzle the sauce from the pie pans around and garnish with fresh basil buds.

MEDITERRANEAN

Journal – Mediterranean

DAY 4 *Embarkation, Barcelona*

Some of us come to the ship more refreshed than others. Particularly those who spent the night ashore dancing and drinking at the Festival del Grec. Barcelona has been thoroughly enjoyed – the medieval Gothic buildings and tiny streets of Barri Goti have been wandered through. Gaudi's curvy masterpieces, Cas Batlio, La Sagrada Familia and La Pedrera wondered at. The Picasso "Blue Period" paintings

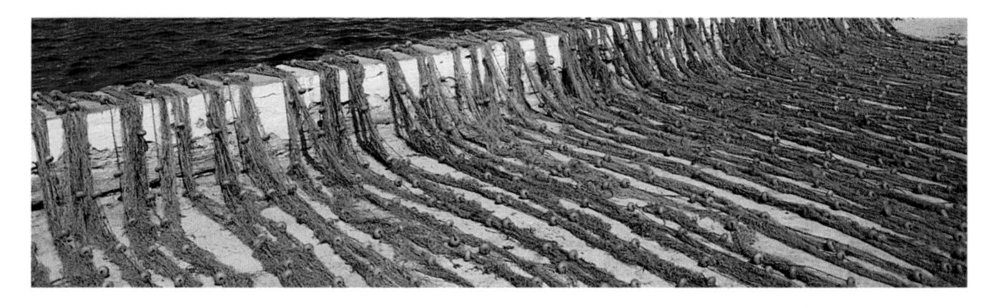

absorbed. And the small-plated tapas sampled – olives (black, green, pickled, and stuffed), anchovies, shrimp in olive oil, fried calamari and the most extraordinary home-cured Spanish ham. The ship is ready for the sun and salt of the Mediterranean, and so are we.

DAY 5 *Port of call, Naples/Capri, Italy*

The ship has sailed in and out of the luxe blue French Rivera waters of Monaco and tacked past Bastia at the top of Corsica's pinnacle. She has drifted by Napoleon's Elba, looked up at the rocky coast of Monte Cristo and scooted within sight of the La Maddalena Archipelago at the north end of Sardinia. This morning, she glides down the Amalfi coast and its rose and honey-colored islands.

Feeling like seasoned yachtsmen (after all, we've been at sea for five days), we hire a motor boat and put-put around the island of Capri to the Green Grotto. The bright sunlight reflects off underwater limestone cliffs and glows with immaculate serenity.

DAY 6 *At sea*

It's when the ship scoots past Italy's big toe, interrupting its kick to Sicily, that the realization hits. This vessel has become home. Only better. Not just because of

ITALIAN TRATTORIA DINNER

APPETIZERS

Prosciutto Crudo di Parma
Sweet Melon and Fresh Fig

Eggplant Parmigiana
Fresh Roma Tomato Sauce

Rustic Vegetable Minestrone
Pesto Crostini

ENTRÉES

Sella di Lepre Arrostito
Chickpea and Dried Fruit Barley

Gamberi alla Frá Diavolo
Brandy Flambé, Pearl Rice and Fiery Tomato Sauce

Branzino Cileno
Risotto al Nero di Seppia, Pinot Grigio Tomato Salad

Vitello allo Scalogno
Roasted Purple Potatoes, Marsala and Shallots

DESSERTS

Zabaglione
A Traditional Warm Italian Dessert

Tiramisu
Espresso, Kahlúa and Mascarpone Cheese

the fine service, splendid activities, heavenly food and ever-changing scenery lazing past the cabin balcony. It's the sense of community, the shared travel experience that hums in the heart. The pleasure of seeing a school of jumping dolphins and turning to a fellow passenger with a smile and a "wow..."

DAY 7 *Port of call, Venice*

1) Driving up the Adriatic Sea into Alpine head winds is a potent, sense-infused experience. Even in bed one can still taste the brisk, salted air and remember the short steep waves with sky pink shimmering in them.

2) Arriving in Venice by water is transcendent, as though the ship is standing still. Out of a fog, the city seems to float toward us, it's Byzantine architecture increasing in size and complexity. Sky, stone and water. Joyous and melancholy. Mysterious.

3) Venetian humanity is evident in their traditional-exotic cuisine, a result of crossroads spice trading with Asian, Turk and Arab tastes. We spend the early evening as Venetians "andar per ombre," stepping from one osteria to another sipping an "ombra" or "shadow" of wine, before landing for supper.

DAY 10 *Port of call, Athens, Greece*

The Plaka, Athens' oldest neighborhood, down below the Acropolis, is explored on foot (a good thing because cars aren't allowed). A small glass of ouzo comes with snacking mezedes, perfect for listening to a sad-faced accordion player. Lunch is a tug of war between lamb fricasee (stew with spinach, lemon, eggs and oil) and the fast food of Greece, souvlaki (rolled pita bread with rotisserie-roasted meat in cucumber-yogurt-garlic sauce). They both win.

DAY 11 *Port of call, Ephesus, Turkey (Kusadasi)*

The ship wends its way through the Greek islands toward Asia Minor settling in at the small fishing port of Kusadasi, Turkey. A tour to the ancient city of Ephesus, now a preserved ruin, provides a contemplative opportunity. Saints Paul and John wrote their letters and gospels here.

Our brightened halos are rewarded with Turkish-prepared tea, ruby-colored and served in delicate clear glasses. And a platter of sweets including Lokmas (fried dough with syrup) and Helvas (pan-sautéed flour and pine nuts with milk and sugar).

The ship departs in the early evening on a northerly course to Istanbul, our final destination. Our appetites satiated, our senses awakened, our souls restored.

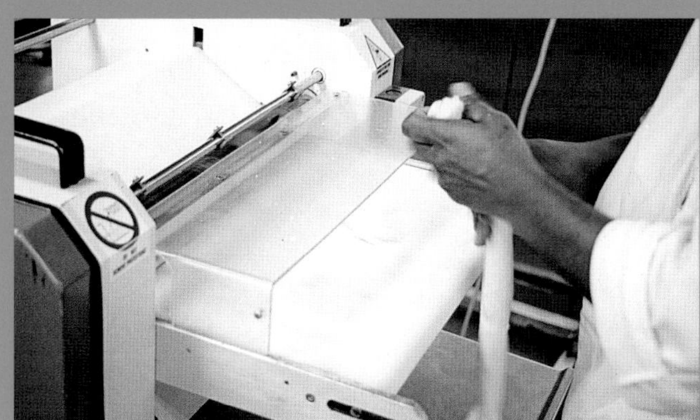

EACH OF OUR 24-HOUR BAKERY OPERATIONS

PRODUCES 9,000 ROLLS BAKED FRESH SIX TIMES DAILY.

PROSCIUTTO CRUDO DI PARMA

Sweet Melon and Fresh Fig

Serves 6

1½ pounds good quality prosciutto

12 melon balls of honeydew

12 melon balls of cantaloupe

3 fresh figs, quartered

PARSLEY-BASIL OIL

½ cup extra virgin olive oil

juice from 1 lemon

2 tablespoons fresh parsley, chopped

2 tablespoons fresh basil, chopped

salt and cracked black pepper

Prosciutto is the Italian word for ham, the best coming from Parma and San Daniele. The ham is salt-cured and air-dried. Prosciutto cotto is cooked while prosciutto crudo is raw, but ready to eat. Prosciutto is best served in very thin slices and paired with mild sweet fruits like melons and figs, with asparagus or hearty lettuces like endive and arugula.

Mix the parsley-basil oil ingredients together, adjust the seasoning and hold at room temperature.

Prepare the melon and figs. Slice the prosciutto as thin as possible. Arrange the prosciutto on plates with the melon and fig and drizzle with the oil.

Add salt and fresh cracked black pepper.

EGGPLANT PARMIGIANA

Fresh Roma Tomato Sauce

Serves 6

FRESH TOMATO SAUCE
(makes 2 cups)

1/4 cup olive oil

4 pounds Roma tomatoes, peeled, seeded and chopped

8 cloves fresh garlic, chopped

2 cups onion, small dice

2 teaspoons sugar

1/4 cup fresh basil, chopped

1/4 cup fresh oregano, chopped

salt and pepper

1 teaspoon butter, cold

6 medium Long Tom eggplants

1 cup mozzarella, shredded

3/4 cup Parmesan, shredded

olive oil for frying

2 garlic cloves

salt and pepper

fresh basil leaves

Preparing the tomato sauce in advance makes this a tasty and quick dish to put together. Seasoning the eggplant well and using good quality cheeses is important. Eggplants are available fresh all year long and any variety may be substituted, including white eggplant. The eggplant can also be sliced, stacked and presented in various ways.

When in season, use fresh Roma tomatoes. Peel them by cutting a small X in the end of the tomato (opposite the stem end). Place the tomatoes in boiling water for approximately 20 seconds. Remove from the boiling water and place into ice water to stop them from cooking. The peel can then be pulled off with your hands or by using a small knife. Cut the tomatoes in half, remove and discard the seeds and the stem end and rough chop. Alternatively, use a good quality canned Roma tomato that has been peeled and seeded.

Heat the olive oil gently in a heavy stock pot. Sauté the onions and garlic until translucent. Increase the heat, add the chopped tomatoes and the sugar. If the tomatoes are very sweet, omit the sugar from the recipe. Stir the tomatoes often to allow for evaporation and prevent burning, approximately 10 minutes. Add the fresh herbs and season with the salt and pepper. Cook 3 more minutes, stir in the cold butter and serve immediately.

Cut the eggplant lengthwise into 1/4-inch slices keeping them connected at the stem end. Salt the sliced eggplants generously and let sit for 15 minutes to draw out moisture. Rinse the salt off and pat the eggplant dry with a paper towel.

Heat the oil in a sauté pan with the garlic cloves to season the oil. Cook the eggplant until tender and nicely browned on each side. Form the eggplant into fans as they are cooking.

Preheat the broiler. Place the cooked eggplant fans on a baking tray. Season with salt and pepper and top with the mozzarella and Parmesan cheeses. Place under the broiler to melt and brown the cheese.

Meanwhile, heat the tomato sauce. Serve the Eggplant Parmesan on a bed of the fresh tomato sauce and garnish with basil leaves.

RUSTIC VEGETABLE MINESTRONE

Pesto Crostini

Serves 10

3 tablespoons olive oil

2 garlic cloves, crushed
½ cup onion, diced
¼ cup white wine

½ cup carrot, diced
½ cup zucchini, diced
⅔ cup tomato, diced
½ cup yellow tomato, diced
¼ cup celery, diced
½ cup yellow squash, diced
⅔ cup garbanzo beans
½ cup white beans
¼ cup green peas
8 cups vegetable stock (p. 221)
3 bay leaves
1¼ cups fresh spinach leaves
salt and pepper

2 tablespoons olive oil

¼ cup basil pesto (p. 74)

1 loaf thick crust baguette
salt and pepper

Parmesan cheese, shaved

The word minestrone is used to describe a hearty soup. These soups are commonly filled with vegetables, meat, beans, rice, pasta or any combination together. They are intended to be robust and satiating. Drizzle a good quality olive oil over the soup and top with Parmesan cheese just before serving.

Pre-cook the garbanzo and white beans or buy a good quality canned product.

Heat the olive oil together with the garlic in a stock pot. Sauté the onion until translucent. Add the wine and evaporate. Add the remainder of the vegetables, except for the spinach, and sweat. Add the stock and bay leaves and cook for approximately 30 minutes until all of the vegetables have softened and the flavors have combined well. Adjust the seasoning and add the spinach leaves a few minutes before serving.

Preheat oven to 400°F. Cut the baguette into thick slices. Brush the slices on both sides with olive oil and season with the salt and pepper. Place on a baking tray and bake until crisp and brown on both sides, turning them at least once. Top each slice generously with the pesto.

Serve in a soup plate. Garnish with the crostini and shaved Parmesan.

SELLA DI LEPRE ARROSTITO

Chickpea and Dried Fruit Barley

Serves 6

6 saddles of rabbit
2 teaspoons fresh sage, chopped
1 teaspoon fresh oregano, chopped
1 teaspoon fresh thyme, chopped
¼ teaspoon fresh rosemary, chopped
salt and pepper
olive oil for frying

BARLEY

1 cup pearl barley
1 tablespoon butter
3 tablespoons onion, chopped
4 cups chicken stock (p. 221)
¼ cup dried papaya, diced
¼ cup dried cranberries
¼ cup dried pineapple
¼ cup dried nectarines
⅓ cup chickpeas, cooked
1 teaspoon fresh thyme, chopped
2 teaspoons fresh mint, chopped
salt and pepper

SAUCE

¼ cup shallots, chopped
1 teaspoon garlic, chopped
⅛ teaspoon powdered mustard
½ cup white wine
¼ cup brandy
1½ cup chicken stock (p. 221)
½ cup demi-glace (p. 220)
½ teaspoon fresh parsley, chopped
salt and pepper

½ pound green French beans
salt and pepper

Barley is the earliest known cultivated cereal grain. It is firm in texture and somewhat mild in flavor and absorbs a tremendous amount of liquid for its size. This is important to remember when adding it to a soup or stew.

Remove the bones from each saddle being careful not to separate the two loins. You may want to request boneless saddles from your butcher. Lay them out flat, skin side down, and season well with the salt, pepper and fresh herbs. Roll the saddles up, each side toward the center, pulling the thin flaps from the sides over the top of the roll. Tie the rolls up firmly with butcher's string. Cover and refrigerate until ready to cook.

Soak the barley the night before in water then drain. Melt the butter and sauté the pearl barley for 4 minutes. Add the chopped onions and sauté until tender. Add half of the chicken stock and simmer the barley uncovered, stirring occasionally. As the liquid is absorbed, add just enough stock a little at a time to keep the barley wet, but not soupy. Once the barley is tender, approximately 40 minutes, add the dried fruits and cooked chickpeas. Simmer 10 more minutes, adding stock as necessary. Stir in the fresh mint and thyme just before serving. Adjust the seasoning.

Heat some olive oil in a large sauté pan and sear the rabbit saddles turning them until well browned. Reduce the heat and continue to sauté until the rabbit is almost cooked, approximately 10 to 12 minutes (the rabbit will cook very much like chicken). Remove the rabbit from the pan and add the chopped shallots to begin the sauce. Sauté until tender then add the garlic and sauté for 2 minutes. Add the mustard. Then deglaze the pan by adding the white wine and brandy and reducing to a syrup while scraping all of the particles from the pan. Add the stock and demi-glace and reduce by half to thicken. Add the chopped parsley and season. Remove the string from the rabbit, place back into the sauce over very low heat and baste the rabbit for a few minutes.

Meanwhile, bring 2 quarts of salted water to a boil. Cook the trimmed beans until just tender, but still crisp. Remove from the water and season.

Remove the rabbit from the sauce and let rest a couple of minutes before slicing. Place the barley in the center of the plates. Drizzle generously with the sauce and arrange the green beans and sliced saddle of rabbit.

GAMBERI ALLA FRÁ DIAVOLO

Brandy Flambé, Pearl Rice and Fiery Tomato Sauce

Serves 6

36 jumbo tiger prawns

1/3 cup brandy

olive oil for frying

salt and pepper

3 cups fiery tomato sauce (p. 219)

2 green peppers

2 red peppers

2 yellow peppers

2 zucchini, thick slice

36 white asparagus spears, trimmed

2 heads radicchio, quartered

1/4 cup olive oil

2 teaspoons garlic, chopped

1 teaspoon fresh oregano, chopped

1 teaspoon fresh marjoram, chopped

salt and pepper

RICE

1 tablespoon butter

1 cup pearl rice

1/4 cup onion, chopped

2 1/2 cups water, chicken or fish stock (p. 221)

1/2 bay leaf

salt and pepper

fresh Italian parsley

Frá Diavolo, or "of the devil" refers to the fiery tomato sauce. Make this dish as spicy as you like with a combination of fresh garlic and chiles. The fiery spice is a welcome contrast to the sweet prawns and aromatic brandy.

Prepare the tomato sauce. Split the tail of the prawns to remove the mud vein. The prawns can be served shell-on or you can remove the shell if desired.

Clean the bell peppers and cut into large strips. Combine all of the vegetables with the olive oil, garlic, herbs, salt and pepper. Toss the vegetables to coat evenly and marinate for approximately 30 minutes.

Brush the prawns with a little oil and season. Heat a sauté pan and gently sauté the prawns 4 to 6 minutes. Just before the prawns are finished, add the brandy and reduce. The brandy may be flamed, but only if the prawns have been peeled, otherwise the shells will burn. Add a couple of spoons of the tomato sauce to the shrimp and toss to coat lightly.

Preheat the grill, broiler, or use a heavy bottom pan on the stove top for the vegetables. They will take approximately 6 minutes to cook and will char a little which is desired.

Meanwhile, melt the butter in a saucepan. Sauté the onions until soft. Add the rice and sauté for 3 or 4 minutes. Add the bay leaf and water or stock. Reduce the heat, cover the pan and cook for approximately 15 minutes. The rice should be soft and moist when cooked. Remove the bay leaf and adjust the seasoning before serving.

Arrange the prawns and vegetables around the rice and serve with a generous portion of the fiery tomato sauce.

BLANCHING IS ONE OF THE METHODS USED TO PREPARE MORE THAN 170,000 POUNDS OF FRESH VEGETABLES EACH MONTH ON THE GRAND PRINCESS®.

BRANZINO CILENO

Risotto al Nero di Seppia, Pinot Grigio Tomato Salad

Serves 6

6, 7-ounce each sea bass filet portions

juice from 2 lemons

seasoned flour for dusting

oil for sautéing

salt and pepper

RISOTTO

6 to 8 cups chicken stock (p. 221)
(water may be substituted)

1½ cups Arborio rice

3 tablespoons olive oil

⅓ cup onion, small dice

½ cup Pinot Grigio, white wine

1 ounce squid ink

juice from half a lemon

¼ cup butter

1 cup Parmesan cheese, grated

salt and pepper

TOMATO SALAD

1 green heirloom tomato

1 yellow heirloom tomato

1 red heirloom tomato

1 orange heirloom tomato

2 tablespoons olive oil

¼ cup Pinot Grigio, white wine

salt and white pepper

1½ pound rapini

1 teaspoon butter

salt and pepper

Squid ink can be purchased in most specialty stores. It is sold dried, frozen and in its natural state in small vacuum packed pouches, which is preferred. The ink has little impact on the flavor of a dish and is primarily used for a dramatic presentation. It should always be added a little at a time near the end of the preparation. Be careful not to spill the ink as it will stain. If squid ink is not available, black food coloring may be used, but do not substitute with any other kind of ink.

Season the fish filets lightly with salt and pepper and squeeze the lemon juice over them. Dredge the filets in the seasoned flour and shake off the excess. Heat the oil in a large sauté pan. Sauté the sea bass over moderately high heat until golden brown on both sides. Reduce the heat and continue to cook until the flesh has firmed and is opaque, approximately 8 minutes.

Meanwhile, bring the chicken stock to a boil. In a separate stock pot, heat the olive oil and sauté the onion until tender. Add the rice and continue to sauté approximately 6 minutes or until the rice has absorbed all of the oil. Add the white wine and allow the rice to absorb it. Add 2 cups of the chicken stock and simmer the rice slowly as it absorbs the stock. Stir the rice to prevent sticking and add remaining stock to the rice a little at a time as it is absorbed until the rice is tender, but has a slight bite to it (al dente). This should take approximately 20 minutes. The rice should be well moistened, but not soupy. Just before serving, stir in the squid ink until a dark black color is formed evenly. Add the fresh lemon juice, butter and the Parmesan cheese and stir well. Season and serve immediately.

Wash the tomatoes and cut them into thin wedges. Toss them together with the olive oil, white wine, salt and pepper and marinate un-refrigerated for 30 minutes.

Wash the rapini and trim the stalks. Steam quickly, approximately 3 minutes, just until tender. Toss the rapini in a little butter, salt and pepper before serving.

When serving, place a fish filet on a generous portion of the risotto. Garnish with the rapini and top with the tomato salad. A sauce should not be required as the moisture of the risotto and the juices from the tomato salad should be enough.

VITELLO ALLO SCALOGNO

Roasted Purple Potatoes, Marsala and Shallots

Serves 6 to 8

1, 7-rib veal rack

salt and pepper

SAUCE

⅔ cup shallots, chopped

6 garlic cloves

½ cup white wine

1 cup Marsala

1½ cups beef stock (p. 220)

½ cup demi-glace (p. 220)

1 teaspoon, fresh sage

¼ teaspoon rosemary

salt and pepper

1 pound baby purple potatoes, sliced thick

6 baby artichokes

6 baby yellow crookneck squash

6 baby zucchini

1 teaspoon butter

juice from a lemon

salt and pepper

All meat items should be seared before roasting. Searing is the act of exposing the surface to high temperature which seals the pores and helps the meat retain its natural juices. This is normally accomplished in a pan on top of the stove. For large pieces of meat the searing process may take place in the oven as in the recipe below by placing the meat in a very high temperature oven for 15 to 20 minutes and then reducing the temperature for the remainder of the cooking process.

Preheat oven to 450°F. Rub the veal rack with salt and pepper. Truss the rack with butcher's string. In a roasting pan, place the veal in the oven. After 15 minutes, reduce the temperature to 325°F and roast for approximately 1 hour longer. The internal temperature should be 135°F.

20 minutes before the veal has finished roasting, season the sliced baby purple potatoes well and add them to the roasting pan to cook. Begin to prepare the vegetables. Trim, halve and remove the choke from the baby artichokes. Squeeze lemon juice over the cut halves to prevent them from turning brown. Trim and clean the baby yellow squash and baby zucchini. Steam the vegetables together until just tender. Toss with butter and season.

Remove the veal from the oven and pour off any excess fat from the roasting pan. The veal rack and potatoes can be kept warm in a low temperature oven. Put the roasting pan on a burner on moderate heat and add the shallots and garlic and brown. Add the white wine and Marsala to the roasting pan and reduce, scraping all of the particles from the bottom of the pan. Add the stock and demi-glace and reduce by half to thicken. Add the herbs and season. The sauce should be rustic and unstrained.

Carve the veal rack as desired and serve with the vegetables, potatoes and sauce.

KIWANO

ZABAGLIONE

A Traditional Warm Italian Dessert

Serves 6

LADY FINGERS

½ cup flour, sifted

½ cup confectioner's sugar, sifted

pinch of salt

2 eggs

2 egg yolks

½ teaspoon vanilla extract

¼ teaspoon almond extract

2 egg whites

castor sugar for dusting

SABAYON

9 egg yolks

⅔ cup confectioner's sugar

½ cup Marsala

½ cup white wine

3 small pomegranates

2 star fruit, sliced

2 kiwanos

Sabayon is easy to prepare and makes a delicious dessert by itself or can be added to cake as a sauce. Although traditionally flavored with Marsala, any desired flavoring or ingredients may be incorporated. The dessert should always be prepared at the last minute so it is served warm and foamy. Because the dessert requires so much whisking, it can be a fun way to get your guests to help out.

Preheat the oven to 375°F. Sift the dry ingredients for the lady fingers together. Whisk the eggs, egg yolks, vanilla and almond extracts together until thickened. Whisk the egg whites to a soft peak. Fold the dry ingredients into the egg yolk mixture. Fold in the egg whites. Place the mixture in a piping bag or cookie press and pipe 3 to 4-inch long fingers onto an ungreased baking tray. Bake 10 to 12 minutes or until dry and light golden brown. Remove from the oven and cool slightly. Dust with castor sugar and finish cooling.

Place the egg yolks and sugar over a double boiler for the sabayon and whisk 10 to 15 minutes until tripled in volume and thickened. Continue to whisk, slowly adding the Marsala and white wine.

Split the pomegranate in half and remove the seeds. Serve the sabayon in the pomegranate shell and garnish with slices of fruit, pomegranate seeds and lady fingers.

TIRAMISU

Espresso, Kahlúa and Mascarpone Cheese

Serves 6 to 8

SPONGE

7 egg yolks

3/4 cup sugar

4 egg whites

1/8 teaspoon salt

3/4 cup flour

1/4 cup cornstarch

FILLING

3 egg yolks

1/3 cup castor sugar

1 1/4 cup mascarpone cheese

3/4 cup double cream

1/2 cup espresso coffee

1/4 cup amaretto

1/4 cup Kahlúa

cocoa powder for dusting

TUILES

1/2 cup unsalted butter

1 teaspoon vanilla extract

1/2 cup confectioner's sugar

3 egg whites

1/2 cup flour

confectioner's sugar for dusting

roasted coffee beans

Mascarpone is a classical Italian double or triple cream cheese. It may be best known as a key ingredient in tiramisu, but is equally suited for savory applications, as seasoned or sweetened spreads, to replace heavy cream in a recipe, or to simply eat as a cheese on its own. Look for fresh ivory colored cheese with a mild aroma and a thick consistency.

Preheat oven to 350°F. For the sponge, cream the egg yolks and sugar together, whisking until doubled in volume. Whip the egg whites to a stiff peak. Gently fold in the egg yolk mixture. Sift the dry ingredients together and gently fold in. Line 2 baking trays with parchment paper and spread the mixture out evenly to a 1/4-inch thickness. Bake for 8 to 10 minutes. The sponge should not become too brown, nor dry out. Once baked, turn the sponge over onto a damp kitchen cloth. Peel off the parchment paper. Divide each into half so that you have 4 sheets.

Mix the espresso, amaretto and Kahlúa together and set aside. For the filling, whisk the egg yolks and sugar together over a double boiler until tripled in volume and thickened. Remove from the heat and cool to room temperature. Whisk the mascarpone, double cream and 2 tablespoons of the espresso mixture together until smooth and then blend into the egg mixture until smooth.

Begin layering the sponge and cream together. Start with a layer of sponge. Using a pastry brush, generously brush the sponge with the espresso mixture. Spread an even layer of mascarpone and repeat the process ending with a layer of mascarpone on the top. Chill the tiramisu for 2 hours. Use a 3-inch ring cutter or a small knife to cut the tiramisu into circles, or any shape desired. Use cocoa powder and a stencil to decorate the top.

For the tuiles, cream the butter, vanilla and sugar together. Whisk the egg whites to a stiff peak. Fold the flour into the butter until smooth and then fold in the egg whites. Chill for 2 hours. Preheat the oven to 400°F. Spread a thin layer of the mixture onto a slightly greased baking tray forming any shape that you desire. Bake approximately 4 minutes or until the tuiles just start to turn brown. They will brown more as they set. The tuiles can be shaped while still warm by laying them over a rolling pin, forming them into muffin pans, or wrapping them around a wooden spoon handle. Dust with confectioner's sugar when cool.

Serve the tiramisu with the tuiles and roasted coffee beans for garnish.

ALASKA

Journal – Alaska

DAY 1 *Sail from Vancouver*

5:30 PM – the summer sun is still high in the sky over this glittering Canadian city. Mountains all around provide a glimpse of great things to come. On-board, spontaneous celebrations break out everywhere. The ship heads up island-dotted Vancouver Sound, into the North.

DAY 2 *Cruising, Inside Passage*

A day of tranquil beauty. Hundreds of quiet inlets and coves. The bluest water ever. And the trees. Everywhere one looks, an ocean of shady evergreens. The smell of salt blends with pine resin. A fine day at sea. An excellent day to become acquainted with the many amenities and pleasures of the ship.

DAY 3 *Port of call, Ketchikan*

The ship docks during breakfast. The day stretches its arms out in welcome. Off to Creek Street to catch the local flavors and bag a few gifts. Tour the old waterfront, hear about the high adventures and misdeeds of the area's early and colorful residents. Excellent local sea food for lunch (what else?). Note: next trip, arrange to go on a deep-sea fishing expedition – after all, this is the "Salmon Capital of the World."

3 PM – the ship sails. Ever north. The ship feeling like home, only better food. The joy of a good dinner, well-served is unequaled. Especially the custard tart with Alaskan rhubarb.

ALASKA WILDERNESS DINNER

APPETIZERS

Smoked Copper River Salmon
Pumpernickel Domino Bread

Dungeness Crab Cake
Whole Grain Mustard and Chives

Reindeer Chili
In a Bread Bowl with Cheddar Cheese

ENTRÉES

Ketchikan Silver Salmon
Cucumber Salad, Red Skin Mashed Potatoes, Corn and Dill Sauce

Poached Weave of Halibut and Salmon
Delicate Spring Leek Sauce

Alaskan King Crab Legs
Lemon and Drawn Butter

Oven-Roasted Spatchcock
Dried Cranberries, Braised Wild Rice and Lima Beans

DESSERTS

Baked Alaska
Trio of Ice Cream, Vanilla Sponge and Burnt Meringue

Rhubarb Custard Tart
Strawberry-Rhubarb Coulis, Opal Basil

DAY 4 *Port of call, Juneau*

Alaska's capital surrounded by a miraculous vista of trees and mountains. Only way to get here, by sea or by air. The long day allows a boat trip to see wildlife in Gastineau Channel and a bus trip to see the Mendenhall Glacier.

Even time for prowling around the relics of Juneau's famous mining community. And a presentation from Libby Riddles, the first woman to win the Iditarod. Nothing is over-programmed – everyone gets to do what they want, the way they want it. The on-board meals are the same. But it's difficult to avoid planning one's dinner before lunch is over.

7:30 PM – the ship steams due north up the huge sound of Chatham Straight into Lynn Canal before making her evening entrance to Chilkoot Inlet. Dinnertime, at last, is here. Decisions, decisions.

10:30 PM – there is something utterly mesmerizing about the quiet purr of the ship's engines at night. The passengers laugh and talk at dinner, they dance at the on-board nightclubs, or they stare at the water as the phosphorescent wake gushes away from the hull. But inside each, they feel the common heartbeat, the pulse of power as it meets the sea.

DAY 5 *Port of call, Skagway*

Morning finds the ship softly creeping up the Taiya Inlet into Skagway – Gateway to the Klondike Gold Rush and home to Liarsville, the historic camp where miners and other legendary characters gathered. Their fascinating tales are told at a hearty Salmon Bake lunch. Then it's off for a scenic "float" through the world-famous Chilkat Bald Eagle Preserve. Later, sightseeing stories are swapped with heli-hike adventurers of the White Pass and Yukon Railroad.

That night, as the ship slips back down the sound, a million stars peg the mirror-flat water.

DAY 6 *Cruising, Glacier Bay*

A thunderous crash of ice and water provides today's wakeup call – a glacier is calving outside. The private balcony provides the perfect "in-robe" viewing platform, and hot coffee to boot. Here, alongside the ship, are the long-imagined classic sights of Alaska. Enormous frozen rivers, dusted with the gravely soil of several centuries, connecting mountain and sea. Chunks of ice mound the bay. A whale sighting is all that's needed. And given.

The slow-setting sun of the midsummer night makes this special day seem to go on forever.

DAY 7 *Cruising, College Fiord*

Ice flows all around the ship, along with porpoises, seals, sea otters and killer whales. This is the Ivy League of glacierdom, Harvard Glacier, Bryn Mawr Glacier, Smith Glacier, on and on – there are sixteen of them! Beyond, a pink alpenglow on the

Chugach Mountains. The interplay of silver water, blue ice, white snow, green tree and black mountain is lively and serene, breathtaking and joyful, all at the same time.

DAY 8 *Port of call, Seward*

Passengers happy and satiated with great food and unforgettable memories, as the ship drops anchor.

Many travelers continue their adventures on land to Princess Wilderness Lodges at the Copper River, Mt. McKinley National Park, Denali National Park and Fairbanks. Some will take the Midnight Sun Express Train with see-it-all Ultimate Dome rail cars and open air observation platforms. Others will go by luxury motor coach to visit some of the five Alaskan National Parks, or go off the beaten path to the Arctic Ocean and Prudhoe Bay. There truly seems to be something for everyone.

All travelers will go home, their senses enlivened and their dreams fulfilled.

SMOKED COPPER RIVER SALMON

Pumpernickel Domino Bread

Serves 8

1, 1 1/2 to 2-pound side smoked salmon

PEAR SLAW

2 cups pear, julienne

1/4 cup walnuts, sliced

1/4 cup green apple, brunoise

juice from 2 limes

1/4 cup fresh mint, chiffonade

1 teaspoon sugar

1/3 cup mayonnaise

salt and white pepper

DOMINO BREAD

1 pound pumpernickel, sliced

1 1/4 cups butter

1/3 cup Farmhouse Cheshire, grated

juice from 1 lime

salt and pepper

lime slices

Pumpernickel, a dark, dense rye bread is manufactured primarily in Germany and Alsace. The bread is baked in a closed container in an oven at low temperatures, resulting in a unique texture. The rich, almost black color is caused by the caramelization of natural sugars during the cooking process. The sweet-sour flavor which is influenced by its sourdough base compliments savory items such as cheeses and seafood.

Remove the skin and blood vein from the smoked salmon and slice very thin. Keep tightly covered with plastic wrap until ready to serve to prevent drying out.

Working quickly, peel and cut the pear and apple and mix with the lime juice to prevent them from browning. Mix together all other ingredients and toss the slaw. Season.

Buy a good quality, firm pumpernickel, pre-sliced. Soften the butter at room temperature and combine with the Cheshire cheese, lime juice, salt and pepper. Layer the pumpernickel and butter mixture beginning and ending with the pumpernickel. Wrap the layered bread with plastic wrap and chill until the butter sets. Slice just before serving.

Place three or four slices of the salmon on each plate. The slices can be cut square or even round for presentation purposes. Top with the pear slaw and garnish with the pumpernickel domino bread and a slice of lime.

DUNGENESS CRAB CAKES

Whole Grain Mustard and Chives

Serves 6

CRAB CAKES

2 pounds crabmeat, cooked

1/3 cup fresh chives, chopped

1 1/2 cups breadcrumbs

2 tablespoons mustard

1/4 cup white wine

juice from 1 lemon

2 eggs

3/4 cup mayonnaise

1/2 teaspoon Worcestershire sauce

6 dashes Tabasco Sauce

salt and pepper

butter for sautéing

TOMATO COMPOTE

1 cup tomato concassé

1/4 cup olive oil

3 tablespoons balsamic vinegar

1 teaspoon garlic, chopped

3 teaspoons fresh chives, chopped

salt and pepper

SAUCE

2 tablespoons shallots, minced

1/4 cup white wine

1/2 cup whole grain mustard

juice from 1 lemon

2 cups heavy cream

2 teaspoons fresh chives, chopped

salt and pepper

Mustard, a common and versatile condiment, was once so prized for its unique flavors and fabled medicinal purposes that mustard making could be a Papal appointment. Today's mustards are ground seeds that have been combined with vinegar, white wine, herbs and spices to create countless varieties. Served as a condiment of its own, as a marinade for meats, or in a unique sauce, mustard is a relatively simple way to add flavor and color to a variety of dishes.

Squeeze any excess moisture out of the crabmeat. Remove a few flakes of meat for garnish. Combine all ingredients for the crab cakes together except for 1/3 of the bread crumbs. Let sit for 30 minutes then adjust the seasoning. Shape the crab into 12 cakes and coat them with the reserved breadcrumbs. Melt the butter in a sauté pan over a moderate heat. Sauté the crab cakes on all sides until golden brown and hot in the center.

Combine all ingredients for the tomato compote together and let sit for 30 minutes to allow the flavors to combine. Pour off any excess liquid and adjust the seasoning before serving. Should be served at room temperature or slightly warmed.

Place the shallots and white wine in a saucepan and reduce until almost dry. Add the mustard and lemon juice and cook for 1 minute. Add the fresh cream and simmer gently reducing the cream by approximately half or until the sauce has thickened to coat a spoon. Add the chives and season.

Serve two crab cakes on each plate with a spoon of the sauce and the tomato compote. Garnish with crab flakes and chives.

REINDEER CHILI

In a Bread Bowl with Cheddar Cheese

Serves 6 to 8

BREAD

1 cup milk

1 1/4 cups water

1 tablespoon butter

1 tablespoon olive oil

2 tablespoons sugar

2 teaspoons salt

1 package active dry yeast

6 2/3 cups flour, sifted

CHILI

2 tablespoons butter

1 1/2 cups onion, small dice

4 garlic cloves, chopped

2 pounds reindeer, ground (venison or beef may be substituted)

3 cups tomato concassé

1/2 cup red wine

1 to 3 fresh green jalapeños

2 cups kidney beans

2 bay leaves

1/2 clove

3 tablespoons chili powder

salt and pepper

2 cups cheddar cheese, shredded

1 cup sour cream

assorted fresh jalapeños

Reindeer is one of the varieties of venison available as wild game and domestically farmed for consumption. Reindeer, along with elk, moose, caribou, and antelope is low in fat and cholesterol and high in flavor. Meat from wild animals is generally tougher and is more suitable for soups, stews, sausages and braises. Game meat that does not go through a long cooking process as in a stew is best served medium-rare to prevent drying out. Reindeer or any game meat can be substituted for beef in most recipes.

Bring the milk to a boil, remove from the heat and add 1 cup of the water, butter, oil, sugar and salt. Dissolve the yeast in the remaining 1/4 cup of water and add it to the mixture. Stir well and let sit 5 minutes. Stir in 4 cups of the flour then transfer to a board and kneed in the remainder of the flour. Form into a large ball and place in an oiled bowl. Turn the dough to oil the surface and cover the bowl with a damp cloth. Set in a warm environment for approximately 1 hour or until the dough has doubled in size. Punch the dough down and divide into 8-ounce balls. Preheat the oven to 400°F. Place the balls at least 4 inches apart onto a lightly greased and floured baking tray. Use a sharp knife to score the dough balls for decoration. Let the dough rise on the tray while the oven preheats. Once the dough has risen by half, place in the oven. Reduce the temperature to 350°F after 10 minutes and bake for approximately 25 minutes more. Cool on a wire rack. Cut the top portion of the ball off to form a lid. Hollow out the bottom to form a bowl. If you prefer a wetter chili, place the bowls in a 200°F oven to dry out.

Melt the butter in a stock pot and sauté the onions until lightly caramelized. Add the garlic and sauté for 2 minutes. Add the ground meat and sauté until well browned. Add the red wine and reduce. Add the tomato concassé and stew for 10 minutes. Add the remainder of the ingredients and cook for 20 minutes more. Remove some of the excess fat from the top of the chili and adjust the seasoning and spice before serving. A little water, stock or tomato juice can be added if you prefer a wetter chili.

Serve the chili in the bread bowl and top with sour cream, cheddar cheese and fresh jalapeños.

KETCHIKAN SILVER SALMON

Cucumber Salad, Red Skin Mashed Potatoes, Corn and Dill Sauce

Serves 6

6, 7-ounce salmon filet portions, skin-on

juice from 2 lemons

salt and pepper

6 whole spring onions

CUCUMBER SALAD

2 large cucumbers, peeled

1/4 cup white wine vinegar

2 tablespoons vermouth

juice from 1 lemon

2 teaspoons fresh dill, chopped

salt and pepper

MASHED POTATOES

2 pounds red bliss potatoes

1/2 cup milk

1/4 cup butter

salt and pepper

CORN SAUCE

2 tablespoons chopped onion

1 teaspoon chopped garlic

1 1/2 cups vermouth

juice from 1 lemon

1 1/4 cups fresh corn

1 1/2 cups fish stock (p. 220)
(if not using fish stock, replace with more cream, not water)

2 cups heavy cream

1 tablespoon fresh dill, chopped

salt and white pepper

Salmon, the king of fish, has a delicate soft flesh which is relatively high in fat and varying in color from light grey through the spectrum of pinks and oranges to an almost blood red. Its moist characteristics make it suitable for almost any cooking method from a light poach to a hearty roast. There are a wide variety of species available from a number of regions. Salmon is best when purchased fresh, but is also available frozen, smoked, canned, pickled and cured.

Preheat a grill. Season the salmon on both sides with salt and pepper and squeeze the juice from one lemon over the filets. Brush the grill with a little oil. Place the salmon on the grill skin-side down first. Turn the salmon to the flesh side after 2 to 3 minutes. Turn the salmon twice more, alternating the angles to achieve diamond grill marks. Squeeze the juice from the second lemon over the cooked filets. The fish should not take more than 8 to 10 minutes to cook. Salmon is best served medium. Trim the spring onions and season. Rub them lightly with oil and grill until just tender and charred.

Slice the cucumbers as thin as possible lengthwise. Toss all of the ingredients together and marinate the cucumber in the refrigerator for 30 minutes. Adjust the seasoning before serving.

Trim the spots off of the red bliss potatoes and remove approximately half of the peel. Put the potatoes in a large pot well covered with cold salted water and bring to a boil. Cook until just tender. Heat the milk and butter in a pan large enough to hold the potatoes. Drain the cooked potatoes and add them to the milk mixture. Use a potato ricer or a hand mixer to mash the potatoes to a fairly smooth texture incorporating air to make them light and fluffy. Season well.

For the sauce, combine the onion, garlic and vermouth in a saucepan and bring to a boil. Reduce the heat and simmer until the liquid has almost formed a syrup. Add the lemon juice and fresh corn and sauté for 4 minutes. Add the fish stock and reduce by half. Add the cream and reduce by half again or until the sauce has reached the desired consistency. Add the fresh dill and adjust the seasoning.

POACHED WEAVE OF HALIBUT AND SALMON

Delicate Spring Leek Sauce

Serves 6

1, 1¼-pound halibut filet, skinless and boneless

1, 1¼-pound salmon filet, skinless and boneless

salt and pepper

1 gallon court-bouillon (p. 10)

LEEK SAUCE

1 tablespoon butter

3 cups leeks, sliced into rings

1 teaspoon chopped garlic

1 small bay leaf

¼ cup brandy

1¼ cups white wine

juice from 1 lemon

1 cup court-bouillon, strained

½ cup buttermilk

1½ cups heavy cream

salt and white pepper

½ pound shiitake mushrooms, sliced

1 teaspoon butter

salt and pepper

6 new potatoes

2 large carrots, turned

2 medium zucchini, turned

2 teaspoons butter

salt and pepper

marjoram buds

Although available in the northern Pacific and Atlantic oceans, the most prized halibut is found off the Alaskan coast. The extremely large flat fish has a firm, bright-white flesh, which is low in fat with a mild flavor. Halibut filets, available fresh or frozen, stand up well to grilling, sautéing and roasting. Halibut cheeks are considered a delicacy in many cultures.

Prepare the court-bouillon and keep at a simmer; preheat the oven to 300°F. Cut the halibut and salmon into strips ½ inch x ½ inch x 6 inches. Divide into even sets of 4 or 5 strips of each kind of fish, ideally coming up with 6 portions. Weave the salmon and halibut together as if making a basket, being sure to trim the sides of each weaved portion so they are more presentable and will cook more evenly. Season with salt and pepper. Butter an oven-proof casserole that is deep enough to cover the fish with court-bouillon. Place the fish into the casserole. Pour enough hot court-bouillon over the fish to cover it. Place the casserole, uncovered in the oven and poach the fish for approximately 8 minutes. Gently remove the fish from the poaching liquid and place on an absorbent kitchen cloth.

To prepare the sauce, sauté the leeks and garlic in the butter over a moderately low heat so as not to brown. Add the bay leaf, brandy and white wine and simmer until the liquid has almost evaporated. Add the lemon juice and the strained court-bouillon and reduce by half. Add the buttermilk and cream and reduce by half again or until the sauce has reached the desired consistency. Remove the bay leaf and adjust the seasoning.

Sauté the mushrooms in the butter over moderately high heat allowing the slices to brown. Season.

Use a small knife to shape the new potatoes into mushroom caps. Place the trimmed potatoes in cold salted water and boil until tender, 8 to 10 minutes.

Clean and peel the carrots and clean the zucchini. Cut the carrots and zucchini into 2½-inch lengths. Quarter the sections and turn them to resemble the shape of a football. Steam or blanch the carrots and zucchini until just tender, 6 to 8 minutes for the carrots and 3 to 4 minutes for the zucchini. Toss all of the vegetables with butter, salt and pepper before serving.

Serve the fish on a bed of the leek sauce and garnish with the potatoes, vegetables, sautéed mushrooms and marjoram buds.

ALASKAN KING CRAB LEGS

Lemon and Drawn Butter

Serves 6

6 pounds king crab legs

DRAWN BUTTER

$1\frac{1}{2}$ pounds unsalted butter

1 to 2 cups crab shells

juice from 1 lemon

1 clove garlic

2 stalks fresh tarragon

$\frac{1}{2}$ teaspoon sugar

salt and white pepper

6 lemons, quartered

King crab, the largest of the crab family is found primarily off the coasts of Alaska and Japan. Its bright red-skinned flesh is delicate, sweet and well worth the trouble it takes to remove the meat from the shell. Other crab varieties include Dungeness, Snow, Blue, Stone and Rock which are just a few of the thousands available. Crabmeat can be used in a variety of recipes and preparations while whole crab is best when simply steamed or boiled.

King crab legs are almost always purchased already cooked. All you have to do is heat them. The best way to accomplish this is by steaming them or alternatively by placing them in boiling water. Crab legs are much more enjoyable to eat if they are served split. This can be done at home with a large sharp knife, but is a little tricky. Many seafood counters at grocers will split them for you. It is well worth it, even if there is a charge. Split crab legs should be steamed only, not boiled, or the flesh will take on too much water.

Place the butter with some scrap crab shells in a saucepan. Squeeze the lemon juice into the butter and then place the squeezed lemon halves into the pan. Add the garlic clove, tarragon and sugar and melt the butter over a very low temperature. If the butter gets too hot, it will brown. Continue to cook over very low heat for 20 minutes, allowing the butter to take on all of the flavors. Remove the white foam and particles from the top of the butter, strain and season before serving.

Serve the crab with the warm drawn butter, fresh lemon, and any assortment of steamed vegetables, potatoes or rice.

OVEN-ROASTED SPATCHCOCK

Dried Cranberries, Braised Wild Rice and Lima Beans

Serves 6

6, 1 to 1½-pound spatchcock

fresh thyme

1 onion

2 carrots

2 celery stalks

12 cloves fresh garlic

salt and pepper

12 baby crookneck squash

WILD RICE

1 cup wild rice

4 cups chicken stock (p. 221) or water

½ cup bacon, chopped

⅔ cup onion, chopped

2 teaspoons garlic, chopped

⅛ teaspoon nutmeg

1¼ cups lima beans, cooked

½ cup demi-glace (p. 220)

salt and pepper

CRANBERRY SAUCE

2 teaspoons shallots, minced

1 teaspoon garlic, minced

1¼ cups dried cranberries

¼ cup white rum

⅔ cup red wine

¼ teaspoon mustard

1½ cups chicken stock (p. 221)

1 cup demi-glace (p. 220)

salt and cracked black pepper

Wild rice, not really rice at all, but a grass seed, has a robust nutty flavor and dense, relatively tough texture. It is expensive, due to its labor-intensive harvesting and limited growing area. The rice should be well washed in cool water and allowed to soak for a few minutes before cooking. Wild rice can be mixed with other white rice varieties in order to break up its dominant characteristics, but should be cooked separately as they will require different lengths of time to become tender.

Preheat the oven to 425°F. Wash the hens and trim off any excess fat. Season the cavities well with thyme, salt and pepper. Rough cut the onion, carrots and celery, peels and all. Add the garlic cloves and stuff the cavities. Truss the hens with butcher's string.

In a roasting pan, place the hens in the oven. After 15 minutes, reduce the temperature to 350°F and roast for approximately 35 to 40 minutes longer until the hens are cooked through. Split the crookneck squash, season and add to the roasting pan for the last 5 minutes. Remove from the oven and let rest a few minutes. Remove the string and the filling from the hens.

Meanwhile, wash the wild rice repeatedly, pouring off any impurities. Bring the stock to a boil and stir in the rice. Simmer uncovered and without stirring for 30 to 40 minutes or until the grains begin to split and the rice is tender. Drain off any excess liquid. In a sauté pan, sauté the bacon until crisp. Add the onions and brown. Add the garlic, nutmeg and lima beans and sauté for 3 minutes. Pour off any excess fat. Add the wild rice and sauté for 5 minutes. Add the demi-glace just to coat the rice well and adjust the seasoning.

In a saucepan, combine the shallots, garlic, cranberries, rum and red wine and simmer to reduce the liquid to a syrup. Add the mustard and chicken stock and reduce by half. Add the demi-glace and simmer 10 minutes or until the sauce has thickened to coat a spoon. Season liberally with black pepper as it is an integral part of the sauce's character.

Serve the hens on a bed of the wild rice with the crookneck squash and a generous amount of the cranberry sauce.

BAKED ALASKA

Trio of Ice Cream, Vanilla Sponge and Burnt Meringue

Serves 8

VANILLA SPONGE
(Makes one 9-inch cake)

6 egg yolks

¾ cup sugar

1 teaspoon vanilla essence

juice from 1 lemon

¼ cup sweet white wine

1¼ cups flour

⅛ teaspoon salt

1 teaspoon baking powder

4 egg whites
(Grated lemon or orange zest can be added. The white wine can be replaced with different flavored alcohol.)

buttermilk-vanilla ice cream (p. 218)

strawberry-Cointreau ice cream (p. 218)

chocolate-rum ice cream (p. 218)

MERINGUE
2 cups sugar

¼ teaspoon cream of tartar

1 cup water

6 egg whites

CHOCOLATE SAUCE
1½ cups water

⅔ cup honey

3 ounces unsweetened chocolate

½ teaspoon vanilla essence

¼ cup brandy

Named for its resemblance to a glacier which has been lightly burnt, Baked Alaska is a unique and surprising dessert with a cool ice cream center and warm meringue crust. The whipped egg whites conduct heat poorly allowing the light sweet meringue to brown before melting the frozen center. While still whole, the dessert can be spritzed with alcohol and flamed.

Begin by preparing the vanilla sponge. Preheat oven to 350°F. Whisk the egg yolks and sugar together over a hot water bath until more than doubled in volume. Add the vanilla, lemon juice and wine and whisk. You want to incorporate as much air as possible. Remove from the water bath and cool. Sift the flour, salt and baking powder together and gently fold into the egg mix. Whisk the egg whites to a stiff peak and gently fold into the mix. Grease and flour the cake pan. Pour the mixture in to fill the pan ⅔ full. Bake for 40 minutes or until a toothpick inserted into the center comes out clean. The sponge should not become too brown, nor dry out. Once baked, cool the sponge on a wire rack. Wrap tightly with plastic wrap if refrigerating.

Prepare the ice creams (any ice cream may be substituted).

In a saucepan, dissolve the sugar and cream of tartar in the water and bring to a boil. Cook covered until a temperature of 240°F is reached, remove from the heat and cool slightly. Meanwhile, whisk the egg whites to a soft peak. Continue to whisk and drizzle in the hot sugar syrup. Whisk the meringue until cool and a medium peak is achieved.

Preheat broiler to 500°F. Begin assembling the Baked Alaska. Any kind of oven-proof casserole or cake pan may be used. Layer the bottom of the casserole with ½ of the sponge cake. Spread the ice cream in three layers filling up the casserole. Top the casserole with another layer of sponge cake. Top all of the exposed surfaces with the meringue. Put the meringue in a piping bag to make decorating easier. Put the casserole under the broiler and brown the meringue, approximately 3 minutes. Do not leave the meringue unattended as it will go from brown to burnt in seconds. Serve at once.

Reduce the water and honey slightly over a moderate heat to form a syrup. Chop the chocolate and melt into the syrup without boiling. Add the vanilla and brandy and cook 5 more minutes without boiling. The sauce will thicken as it cools.

Decorate the plates with chocolate sauce and top with a slice of the Baked Alaska. Edible flowers or dried strawberries can be used for garnish.

RHUBARB CUSTARD TART

Strawberry-Rhubarb Coulis, Opal Basil

Serves 6

PÂTE SUCRÉE (SWEET PASTRY)

¼ cup sugar

¼ cup brown sugar

⅛ teaspoon salt

⅓ cup unsalted butter

1 cup flour, sifted

1 tablespoon heavy cream

1 egg yolk

RHUBARB

2 cups water

2 cups sugar

7 cups rhubarb, sliced

CUSTARD

1½ cups whole milk

1 vanilla bean

½ cup sugar

¼ cup flour

4 egg yolks

STRAWBERRY-RHUBARB COULIS

1 cup fresh strawberries

1 teaspoon fresh orange juice

1 teaspoon fresh lemon juice

1 cup rhubarb, reserved from above

3 tablespoons rhubarb syrup, reserved from above

anglaise sauce (p. 44)

⅛ teaspoon ground anise

fresh opal basil leaves

Sweet pastry is a very versatile dough. It should be refrigerated and worked with in small quantities as it becomes too soft to handle when warmed to room temperature. Rolling the dough between sheets of wax or parchment paper will also help to move the dough once it is rolled to the desired thickness. Refrigerate again in pan or mold to reduce shrinking during baking.

Cream the sugar, salt and butter together. Work in the flour until crumbly. Mix the cream and egg together and combine into the flour mixture. Kneed the dough slightly so it holds together, cover and refrigerate until well chilled. Roll the dough out to ⅛-inch thick and line 6, 4-inch tartlet pans. Chill again.

Bring the water and sugar to a boil and then reduce to a simmer. Place the rhubarb slices in the syrup and cook for 3 minutes. Remove the rhubarb and reserve the syrup.

To prepare the custard, bring the milk and vanilla bean just to the boiling point. Meanwhile, mix the sugar, flour and egg yolks together to form a smooth paste. Remove the vanilla bean from the milk and slowly mix the milk into the paste mixture. Scrape the seeds from the vanilla bean and add to the mixture. Place the tartlets on a baking tray and pour the custard into the chilled tart shells, filling them just to the top.

Preheat the oven to 350°F. Reserve one cup of the rhubarb for the sauce. Lay the remaining rhubarb slices across the top of the custard in a fan pattern. Lightly brush the top with some of the rhubarb syrup and bake for 15 to 20 minutes or until the crust has browned and the custard has set. Remove from the oven and cool on a rack. Brush the tops once more with the rhubarb syrup just before the tarts have completely cooled.

To prepare the coulis, clean the strawberries, cut into pieces and marinate with the orange and lemon juice. Combine with the rhubarb and syrup and blend until smooth in a food processor or blender; do not strain. Add a few more drops of syrup if the sauce is too thick.

Prepare the anglaise sauce, adding the ground anise to the recipe.

Place a tart in the center of the plate and decorate around the tart with the two sauces. Garnish with opal basil.

AUSTRALIA
NEW ZEALAND
SHOPPING
FIORDLANDER I

Journal – Australia/New Zealand

DAY 3 *Port of call, Melbourne, Australia*

On the chart, Melbourne looks to be just around the corner from Sydney. In Australia distances are deceiving. Victoria (the state we are sailing alongside) is as big as Great Britain. We round Point Lonsdale and enter Port Phillip Bay, heading up along Queenscliff toward the apex of the diamond that is Melbourne. It takes a while because the bay is huge. We dock near the Yarra River, which comes down the

city centre to meet the sea. From here, the city doesn't look so big – but then it must have something to do with all that space around it. Australia is Texas supersized a dozen times over.

DAY 5 *Port of call, Hobart, Tasmania*

It's taken a full day to escape Australia's gravity and fly off to its southeast moon, Tasmania. The ship comes around the goatee-shaped island to its scraggly chin where the capital, Hobart is located. Somewhere on their way across the windy Southern Ocean to this harbor is a fleet of sailboats competing in the famously grueling Sydney to Hobart Yacht Race.

We stroll the old architecture streets soaking up the cultural residue left by the colonial Brits and the Aboriginal people who preceded everyone else.

DAY 8 *Cruising, Fiordland, New Zealand*

South Island's greenery glitters in the January summer sun. Milford Sound, situated at the top of Fiordland, draws the ship like a magnet into its deep folds. Dark mountains, water falling everywhere, glide with power and grace down to the night blue bays and coves below. What strikes the senses the most, though, is the quiet – sound seems to be muffled by the cushiony hills or absorbed by the mystical energy that occupies this place.

As the ship ever so slowly makes its turn to leave for Dunedin on the east side of New Zealand, fellow passengers are mesmerized by something high up in the hollow of a cove. A waterfall's descending stream is making a strange U-turn – sending the water up, not down. A moment later, we feel the strong updraft, a reverse williwaw.

CAPTAIN'S GALA DINNER

APPETIZERS

A Symphony of Caviar
Sevruga, Golden and Salmon

Tender Baby Spinach Salad
Applewood-Smoked Bacon and Red Wine Vinaigrette

Cream of Porcini Soup
Sautéed Wild Mushrooms

ENTRÉES

Potato-Crusted Shark Filet
Spinach, Petite Vegetables and Chive Cream

Broiled Lobster Tail
Drawn Lemon-Lobster Butter, Saffron Rice Pilaf

Royal Pheasant in Pan Juices
Butternut Squash, Parisienne Potato Nest, Périgueux Sauce

Châteaubriand
Bouquettière of Classical Garnishes

DESSERTS

Vanilla Cognac Soufflé
Warm Grand Marnier Sauce

Chantilly Swans
Vanilla Cream and Chocolate Mocha Sauce

A SYMPHONY OF CAVIAR

Sevruga, Golden and Salmon

Serves 6

6 ounces sevruga caviar

6 ounces golden caviar

6 ounces salmon caviar

4 eggs

1 large bunch fresh parsley, chopped

1 small red onion, minced

6 Roma tomatoes

1 lemon, sliced

ADDITIONAL CONDIMENTS

1 cup sour cream or crème fraîche

1/3 cup capers, chopped

BLINI

2 cups milk

1 ounce fresh yeast
(1 1/2 teaspoons dry yeast)

1 1/2 cups flour, sifted

1 tablespoon sugar

3 egg yolks

1/2 cup buckwheat flour

1/2 teaspoon salt

2 tablespoons butter, melted

3 egg whites

Caviar is one of the world's greatest and most expensive delicacies originating from the sturgeon species of fish native to the Caspian Sea. The eggs should be plump and shiny and are high in vitamin B12, cholesterol and sodium. A large part of making caviar a delicacy is in the way it is eaten. The numerous classical condiments are served individually so the connoisseur can experiment with different combinations. Caviar should be eaten with a gold, bone or plastic spoon only, as other metals and materials react negatively with the oils in the eggs.

Prepare all of the condiments. Bring the eggs to a boil in cold, salted water. Once boiling, continue cooking for an additional 8 minutes. Run the eggs under cool water when cooked. Peel the eggs and separate the whites from the yolks. Chop each separately.

Wash and chop the parsley. Use a small sharp knife to remove the skin from the Roma tomatoes in one piece. Roll the tomato skin up to form a rose.

For the blini, warm the milk slightly, not to exceed 85°F. Combine the milk, yeast, flour and sugar together until well mixed. Cover and set in a warm place and allow to ferment for 1 hour.

Mix in the egg yolks, buckwheat flour and salt to the fermented batter. Drizzle in the melted butter and mix well. Allow to ferment again for 1 hour.

Whisk the egg whites to a stiff peak and fold into the batter. Heat a non-stick sauté pan over moderate heat. Cook the blini like miniature pancakes in a little butter, browning on each side.

Present the caviars on plates garnished with the various condiments and accompanied by the warm blini.

TENDER BABY SPINACH SALAD

Applewood-Smoked Bacon and Red Wine Vinaigrette

Serves 6

SALAD

1½ pounds baby spinach leaves

2 eggs

8 slices applewood-smoked bacon

1½ cups fresh button mushrooms, washed and sliced

¼ red onion, diced

DRESSING

¾ cup olive oil

¼ cup bacon fat

juice from 1 lemon

½ cup red wine vinegar

1 teaspoon garlic, chopped

2 teaspoons Dijon mustard

1 teaspoon sugar

salt and pepper

Spinach leaves make a great alternative or addition to lettuce in a fresh salad. There are many varieties ranging in size, shape, texture and flavor which can be mixed together to give the salad greater interest. Spinach leaves are generally dirty and should be thoroughly washed in cold water and well drained before use. Mediterranean, African and Asian markets also offer many different and delicious varieties of fresh spinach.

Trim and wash the spinach leaves and allow to drain between damp paper towels.

Bring the eggs to a boil in cold, salted water. Once boiling, cook for an additional 8 minutes. Run the eggs under cool water when cooked. Peel the eggs and separate the whites from the yolks. Chop each separately.

Cook the bacon until crisp. Reserve the bacon fat and chop the bacon.

Combine all of the dressing ingredients in a food processor and blend until fairly smooth. A temporary emulsion should form. Adjust the seasoning and hold at room temperature. Stir the dressing well again before serving and adjust the seasoning once more. The dressing should be made at least 30 minutes before use to allow the flavors to combine. Extra dressing can be refrigerated for future use.

To serve, toss the spinach leaves in a very light coating of the dressing and season lightly with salt and pepper. Arrange the leaves on plates and garnish with the egg, bacon, mushrooms and onion.

Crumbled blue cheese makes a nice addition to this salad.

SHERRY

CREAM OF PORCINI SOUP

Sautéed Wild Mushrooms

Serves 6 to 8

3 tablespoons butter

½ cup onion, diced

¼ cup leek, diced

½ cup celery, diced

½ pound button mushrooms, sliced

½ pound porcini mushrooms, sliced

4 ounces shiitake mushrooms

4 ounces morel mushrooms

4 ounces chanterelle mushrooms

4 ounces oyster mushrooms

¼ cup dry sherry

1 cup potatoes, peeled and diced

3 cups chicken or vegetable stock (p. 221)

2 cups fresh cream

2 tablespoons tarragon, chopped

1 tablespoon parsley, chopped

salt and pepper

nutmeg

tarragon sprigs

Although the flavors of most mushrooms complement each other, some are more overpowering than others. Prices vary greatly and the more exotic varieties can be quite expensive. Button mushrooms are ideal for the base of a soup or sauce. The more exotic mushrooms such as morel (one of the most costly and pungent in flavor and color), chanterelle, porcini, shiitake, and oyster are used to influence the flavor and provide texture and visual appeal to the dish with their unusual shapes.

Melt the butter in a stock pot. Add the onions, leeks and celery and sauté over a moderate heat until the vegetables are tender and slightly translucent. Do not brown the vegetables. Reserve 6 or so pieces of each mushroom variety to be used later as garnish. Add the remainder of the mushrooms to the vegetables and sauté for approximately 10 to 12 minutes or until the mushrooms have softened and most of the water has evaporated. Add the sherry and reduce. Add the potatoes and stock and simmer uncovered until all of the vegetables are tender.

Allow the soup to cool slightly so it can be handled without burning yourself. Using a blender, food processor or stick mixer, puree the soup. The soup should not be perfectly smooth, but should be palatable. Return the soup to the stock pot.

Using a whisk, slightly whip the cream until frothy. Return the soup to the stove. Add the cream and gently bring the soup to a simmer. Add the chopped tarragon and parsley and season with the salt, pepper and a touch of nutmeg.

Sauté the reserved mushroom pieces in a small amount of butter until tender and golden. Season with salt and pepper. Fill soup cups or bowls and arrange the sautéed mushroom pieces floating on the soup with a sprig of fresh tarragon.

Note: Frozen or canned mushrooms may be used in place of fresh, but fresh are preferred. Varieties of mushrooms may be substituted in any combination by others which are more readily available.

POTATO-CRUSTED SHARK FILET

Spinach, Petite Vegetables and Chive Cream

Serves 6

2, 1-pound shark loins, skinless
1/4 cup butter

1 pound spinach leaves
3 large potatoes
salt and pepper
oil for frying

1 head broccoli
1 medium yellow squash
1 medium green zucchini
1 medium carrot
18 spears asparagus
2 teaspoons butter
salt and pepper

chive sauce (p. 221)

Although there are many available species of shark, Mako is preferred. The filet is dense, low in fat, and has a tendency to be dry. Soak the meat in a mild brine or in milk for about two hours before cooking to help neutralize its slightly metallic and ammoniac characteristics.

Begin by preparing the shark loins. Ideally you will have two loins approximately 10 inches long and 3 inches in diameter. They should be soaked 8 hours in lightly salted water. Remove them from the salted water, rinse and dry with an absorbent cloth. Rub the loins with the cold butter and lightly season. Blanch the spinach leaves very quickly in boiling water, then chill in ice water. Squeeze out the excess water and separate the leaves onto paper towels.

Wash and peel the potatoes. Use a regular or a Japanese mandoline to shred the potatoes into very fine strips. A box grater may also be used. Do not shred the potatoes into water.

Working quickly, lay out two pieces of plastic wrap approximately 2-foot square each. Divide the potatoes onto the two sheets of plastic forming 1/2-inch layers slightly longer than the shark loins and wide enough to wrap around the loin. Lightly season the potatoes. Divide the spinach leaves up making uniform layers over the potatoes. Lightly season the spinach. Place one shark loin in the center of each and roll them up forming a layer of spinach and potato around each loin. The potato may seem a little messy at this point, but it will form into place as it cooks.

Preheat the oven to 350°F. Heat a large non-stick pan with a 1/2-inch of oil on the stove top. Carefully remove the plastic wrap from the loins and place them in the hot oil. Do not turn the loins until the side in the pan is well browned. Once the loins are browned on all sides, transfer them to a baking tray and bake for approximately 12 minutes or until the center of the shark loins have turned opaque and firm. Remove from the oven and let rest a few minutes. Season.

Wash and trim the vegetables forming petite diamonds, ovals, spears and florets. Steam the vegetables quickly for 3 to 4 minutes. Toss in the butter and season.

Use a serrated knife to slice the shark. Place two medallions on each plate and create a border with the chive sauce. Arrange the vegetables in alternating colors and garnish with garlic chives or spring onion.

BROILED LOBSTER TAIL

Drawn Lemon-Lobster Butter, Saffron Rice Pilaf

Serves 6

12, 4-ounce Maine lobster tails, or 6, 8-ounce tails

2 tablespoons butter

juice from 1 lemon

1/3 cup white wine

salt and white pepper

DRAWN BUTTER

1 1/2 pounds unsalted butter

1 to 2 cups lobster shell pieces

juice from 1 lemon

1 clove garlic

1/8 teaspoon paprika

1/8 teaspoon cayenne pepper

RICE

12 threads saffron

2 1/2 cups water, chicken or fish stock (p. 221)

1 tablespoon butter

1/4 cup onion, chopped

1 cup jasmine rice

3 tablespoons Pernod

1/2 bay leaf

salt and pepper

3 cups snow peas

1 teaspoon butter

salt and pepper

3 lemons, halved in star shape

fresh chervil

Lobster, the most sought-after shellfish, is pricy but delicious. The meat is tender, slightly sweet and plentiful. The lobster should be purchased whole while still alive or as frozen tails. The most common lobsters to the United States are the Northern Maine lobster and the Caribbean Spiny or Rock lobster. Both are excellent, however, the Caribbean variety has no claws. Lobster is very delicate and should be prepared the day it is purchased live, or if frozen, it should be defrosted in the refrigerator over-night and prepared the next day.

To prepare the drawn butter, place the butter with the lobster pieces in a saucepan. Squeeze the lemon juice into the butter and then place the squeezed lemon halves in the pan. Add the garlic clove, paprika and cayenne and melt the butter over a very low temperature. If the butter gets too hot, it will brown. Continue to cook over very low heat for 20 minutes, allowing the flavors to combine. Remove the white foam and particles from the top of the butter and strain before serving.

Preheat the broiler to 500°F. Split the back of the lobster tails halfway through the meat. Pull the meat out over the top of the shell without detaching it completely and wash the meat with cool water, removing any mud vein.

Arrange the tails uniformly on a broiler pan. Brush each tail with butter and top with the fresh lemon juice, white wine and seasoning. Broil for 6 to 8 minutes depending on the size of the tails. The lobsters are cooked as soon as the meat turns opaque and firm. Overcooking the lobster will make it very tough.

Meanwhile, prepare the rice by placing the saffron in the cold water or stock and allowing it to steep. While it is steeping, melt the butter in a saucepan. Sauté the onions until soft. Add the rice and sauté for 3 or 4 minutes. Add the Pernod and allow the rice to absorb it. Add the stock, bay leaf and the saffron liquid and bring to a boil. Reduce the heat, cover the pan and cook for approximately 20 minutes. The rice should be soft and moist when cooked. Remove the bay leaf and adjust the seasoning before serving.

Trim and clean the snow peas and steam for 3 to 4 minutes until bright green and still crisp. Toss with butter, salt and pepper.

Serve the lobster with the rice and peas, plenty of fresh lemon, the lemon-lobster butter and fresh chervil.

ROYAL PHEASANT IN PAN JUICES

Butternut Squash, Parisienne Potato Nest, Périgueux Sauce

Serves 6

6 breasts of pheasant
2 teaspoons butter
salt and pepper

SAUCE
2 tablespoons shallots, minced
½ cup white wine
¼ cup brandy
1½ cups chicken stock (p. 221)
½ cup demi-glace (p. 220)
¼ cup truffle peelings, chopped
1 tablespoon fresh parsley, chopped
salt and pepper

SQUASH
1, 2 to 3-pound butternut squash
2 tablespoons butter
1/4 teaspoon truffle oil
nutmeg
salt and pepper

POTATOES
4 large potatoes, washed and peeled
oil for frying
1 teaspoon butter
fresh parsley, chopped
salt and pepper

VEGETABLES
1 to 3 teaspoons butter
6 baby carrots, peeled
6 baby marrow
6 yellow patty pans
1 cup small oyster mushrooms
splash of white wine
salt and pepper

Pheasant is widely considered a premium bird due to its size, mild flavor and tender flesh. Other popular feathered game that would be suitable for substitution are partridge, woodcock, grouse and quail.

Heat the butter in a large sauté pan. Season the breasts well and sear in the butter browning both sides. Reduce the heat and cook for 4 minutes. Remove the breasts from the pan just before they have finished cooking.

Begin making the sauce by adding the shallots to the pan in which the pheasant was cooked and sauté until tender and lightly colored. Add the white wine and brandy and reduce by half. Add the chicken stock and reduce by half. Add the demi-glace and reduce until the sauce lightly coats a spoon. Place the breast back into the sauce. Reduce the sauce to a light simmer, being careful not to boil the pheasant. Baste the breasts with the sauce until the breasts have finished cooking. Remove the breasts from the sauce and add the truffle and parsley.

Meanwhile, preheat the oven to 375°F. Cut the squash in half and remove the seeds. Place the squash halves, skin side up on a baking tray and bake for 45 minutes to an hour or until the flesh is soft. Remove from the oven, scoop out the flesh from the skin and place in a bowl with the butter, truffle oil and nutmeg. Season and mix well.

Use a parisienne scoop to form 18 to 24 potato balls. Place the parisienne potatoes in cold salted water and bring to a boil. Cook until just tender. Drain, toss in the butter and parsley, and season.

Heat 3 cups of oil in a fryer or small pan. Prepare the baskets by shredding the potatoes that were scooped out. The easiest way to create the baskets is with a potato basket maker. Fill the bottom basket with shredded potato, but not too much. Close the top basket and carefully place the basket in the hot oil. Fry until golden brown. Gently remove the potato basket from the basket maker, drain on a paper towel and season. The baskets can be made using two ladles, but practice will be necessary.

Heat the butter in a small sauté pan. Split the baby marrow, baby carrots, patty pans and oyster mushrooms in halves. Sauté the vegetables in the butter, beginning with the carrots and then adding the squash and the mushrooms. Add more butter as necessary. Splash the vegetables with the white wine and season well.

Slice the pheasant breast and arrange with the vegetables, squash, potatoes and sauce.

CHÂTEAUBRIAND

Bouquettière of Classical Garnishes

Serves 6

ROAST

2, 1½-pound beef tenderloins, center cut

salt and pepper

oil for searing

6 slices brioche or white bread

BÉARNAISE SAUCE

⅓ cup white wine

2 tablespoons tarragon vinegar

2 teaspoons shallots, chopped

4 white peppercorns

1 sprig fresh tarragon

4 egg yolks

1 cup butter, clarified

2 tablespoons fresh tarragon, chopped

salt and pepper

TOMATO CLAMART

3 Roma tomatoes

1 cup sweet peas

salt and pepper

CHÂTEAU POTATOES

3 large potatoes, washed and peeled

3 tablespoons oil

1 teaspoon butter

fresh thyme, chopped

salt and pepper

CELERY À LA CRÈME

½ teaspoon garlic

¼ cup white wine

Despite its French name, Châteaubriand actually originated in England and features the meat sliced from the center and best part of the tenderloin of beef. The slow-roasted meat should be served with no less than ten accompaniments of classically prepared vegetables and starches, individually arranged and presented tableside on a silver tray.

Preheat the oven to 350°F. Heat a large sauté pan on the stove top with a small amount of oil. Season the tenderloins well and sear on all sides. Transfer to a baking tray and roast in the oven for approximately 25 minutes or until the internal temperature has reached 135°F for rare beef. Once cooked, remove from the oven and let rest before carving.

Cut the bread slices into trimmed squares and place in the oven to brown. Turn at least once to brown on both sides.

Béarnaise Sauce: place the white wine, vinegar, shallots, peppercorns and tarragon sprig in a saucepan. Bring to a boil then reduce to half its volume. Place the egg yolks in a bowl over a double boiler. Whisk the yolks until warm and slightly thickened. Strain the reduction liquid into the egg yolks, whisking continuously. Slowly whisk in the clarified butter. A frothy sauce of mayonnaise consistency should form. Season the sauce and add the chopped fresh tarragon. The sauce can be thinned out with a few drops of warm water if necessary. The sauce must be kept in a warm place. It will separate if it gets too hot or too cold.

Tomato Clamart: bring 1 quart of salted water to a boil. Trim the tops and bottoms off of the Roma tomatoes and plunge into the boiling water for 1 minute to loosen the skin. Remove the tomatoes from the water and peel off the skin. Cut the tomatoes in half and scoop out the seeds. Blanch the sweet peas in boiling water for 3 to 4 minutes. Drain the peas and season. Season the tomato halves and fill each half with the sweet peas.

Château Potatoes: cut the potatoes into quarters. Use a small knife to shape each quarter into a football shaped potato. Heat a non-stick pan with the oil and butter together. Add the potatoes and sauté until well browned and tender. Season with salt, pepper and fresh chopped thyme.

½ bay leaf

1½ cups celery batonnet

1¼ cups heavy cream

⅛ teaspoon truffle oil

salt and pepper

12 slices summer truffle

DUCHESSE POTATOES

2 pounds potatoes, washed and peeled

¼ cup butter

2 egg yolks

nutmeg

salt and pepper

DAUPHINOISE POTATOES

2 cups milk

2 cups heavy cream

1 tablespoon garlic, chopped

8 eggs

nutmeg

cayenne pepper

salt and pepper

3 pounds potatoes, washed and peeled

1 cup Parmesan cheese, grated

12 spears green asparagus

12 spears white asparagus

12 ears baby corn

1 cup chanterelle mushrooms

½ cup tomato concassé

glazed carrots (p. 100)

tarragon

Celery à la Crème: place the garlic, white wine and bay leaf in a shallow pan and reduce to a syrup. Add the cream and reduce by half. Add the celery to the cream and simmer for 3 minutes, stirring often, until the celery just begins to soften. Add the truffle oil and season. Garnish with the sliced truffle.

Duchesse Potatoes: preheat the oven to 425°F. Peel the potatoes and cut in half. In a pot on the stove top, place the potatoes in 1 gallon of salted water and bring to a boil. Boil for 15 to 20 minutes until the potatoes are just tender. Strain and mash with a potato ricer. Mix in the butter, egg yolks, nutmeg and seasoning. Put the potato into a piping bag and pipe shapes onto a buttered baking tray. Brush the shaped potatoes with a little beaten egg and bake a few minutes until browned.

Dauphinoise Potatoes: preheat the oven to 375°F. Combine the milk, cream, garlic, eggs, nutmeg, cayenne, salt and pepper together and mix well. This mixture should be heavily seasoned as the potatoes will absorb much of it. Slice the potatoes ⅛-inch thick. Butter a 12-inch casserole. Layer the potatoes neatly into the casserole. Pour the mixture over allowing the liquid to fill all of the voids. The mixture should rise just to the top of the potatoes, but not submerge them completely. Sprinkle the top of the potatoes with the Parmesan cheese. Wrap the casserole in foil and place in the oven for 40 minutes. Remove the foil and continue to bake 15 to 20 minutes more until the potatoes are tender and well browned. Cut the potatoes into diamonds or any shape desired.

Prepare the asparagus and baby corn by blanching or steaming them for 4 to 5 minutes until just tender. Sauté the mushrooms and tomato concassé separately in a little butter. Season all of the vegetables well.

Prepare the glazed carrots as on (p. 100) using turned or baby carrots.

Presentation: the beauty of this wonderfully classic dish is in its presentation. Arrange the beef and many accompaniments on a large tray. Present the tray at the table and then serve each guest, or place the tray in the center of the table and allow them to serve themselves.

VANILLA COGNAC SOUFFLÉ

Warm Grand Marnier Sauce

Serves 8

SOUFFLÉ

1 cup flour, sifted

1/4 cup cornstarch

1/2 cup sugar

1/4 teaspoon salt

1/2 cup butter

10 egg yolks

2 vanilla beans

5 cups milk

1/4 cup cognac

10 egg whites

GRAND MARNIER SAUCE

1/2 cup sugar

6 egg yolks

2 1/2 cups milk

1/4 cup Grand Marnier

1/8 cup cognac

Soufflés are tasty and impressive desserts to serve to your guests. The preparation is fairly easy; it is the temperamental baking that can cause some stress. This is usually cured with a little practice and learning how your oven performs in combination with your climate. Once you have worked out the timing issues, you can then experiment with a wide variety of flavors for your creations. Soufflés also make excellent appetizers when paired with savory ingredients. Cheese soufflés make a good dessert alternative in place of something sweet.

Preheat the oven to 375°F. Prepare 8, 4-inch oven proof soufflé dishes. Butter the bottom and insides of the dishes well. Coat the buttered surface with sugar.

Cream the flour, cornstarch, sugar, salt, butter and egg yolks together gently without incorporating too much air. Meanwhile, split and scoop out the vanilla bean, add to the milk and bring just to a boil. Slowly add the hot milk into the egg mixture until it is well combined. Return the mixture to a moderate heat and continue to cook until well thickened, do not boil the custard or it will curdle. Remove from the heat, strain and cool. Stir the cognac into the mixture. Whisk the egg whites until stiff, but not dry. Gently fold the egg whites into the mixture. Fill the soufflé cups to 1/2-inch from the top. Place the soufflés in the oven and bake approximately 25 minutes until the soufflés have doubled in size, browned and firmed slightly. Disturb the soufflés as little as possible while baking, especially in the first 15 minutes.

Prepare the sauce by creaming the sugar and egg yolks together. Bring the milk to a boil and slowly add the hot milk into the egg mixture. Add the Grand Marnier and cognac. Return to a moderate heat and cook approximately 10 minutes until it thickens enough to coat the spoon well. Do not allow the sauce to boil.

The soufflé has to be served immediately once cooked. Dust the soufflés with confectioner's sugar and serve with the warm sauce on the side. When eating with the sauce, split the top of a soufflé and pour a little directly into the center.

This recipe can be used as a base to add different liqueurs, flavors, nuts, candied fruits, chocolate, etc.

CHANTILLY SWANS

Vanilla Cream and Chocolate Mocha Sauce

Serves 6

CHOUX PASTE

1 1/2 cups water

1/2 cup unsalted butter

1 1/2 cups flour, sifted

1/8 teaspoon salt

6 fresh eggs

CHANTILLY CREAM

1 3/4 cups heavy cream

1/4 teaspoon vanilla essence

4 tablespoons confectioner's sugar

CHOCOLATE MOCHA SAUCE

1 1/2 cups water

2/3 cup honey

4 ounces unsweetened chocolate

1/2 teaspoon vanilla essence

1/3 cup espresso or strong coffee

1/4 cup dark rum

1/4 teaspoon butter

fresh mint leaves

raspberries

Choux paste is relatively simple and versatile. The batter can be used to form a great variety of shapes. Its neutral flavor lends itself well to use in appetizers, soups, salads, accompaniments to entrées and most popularly, for desserts. Once baked, choux paste holds up well to freezing when tightly wrapped. Allow to thaw completely before unwrapping or it will draw moisture and become soft.

Bring the water and butter to a boil. Add the flour and salt all at once and stir vigorously with a wooden spoon. Reduce the heat and continue to stir until the mixture is a smooth paste and pulls away from the side of the pan. Remove the pan from the heat and allow to cool slightly for approximately two minutes. Add the eggs one at a time stirring well to incorporate. The mixture should be smooth and stiff. Let cool to room temperature.

Preheat the oven to 400°F. Place 1/4 of the mixture in a small piping bag with a small plain tip. Pipe the shape of a backwards S onto the baking tray to form the head and neck. Pipe a few extra to allow for breakage. Place the remainder of the pastry in a piping bag with a medium sized star tip. Pipe 12 egg-sized balls of mixture, onto a separate buttered baking tray. Leave at least 2 inches of space in between each ball for expansion during baking.

Place the trays in the oven at 400°F. The neck pieces will bake in approximately 5 minutes, remove once browned and firm. Bake the balls for the body approximately 5 minutes more, then reduce the temperature to 350°F and continue to bake 10 to 12 minutes. The bodies should be golden brown, dry and firm to the touch. Remove from the oven and cool on a rack.

Whisk the cream, vanilla and sugar together to a medium peak. Taste and adjust the sweetness. Place the cream in a piping bag with a medium star tip.

Prepare the sauce by reducing the water and honey slightly over a moderate heat to form a light syrup. Chop the chocolate and melt into the syrup without boiling. Add the vanilla, espresso coffee and rum and cook 5 more minutes without boiling. Remove from the heat and stir in the small piece of butter and continue to cool. The sauce will thicken as it cools.

To create the swans, cut off the top half of the body using a serrated knife, then split the top piece in half for the wings. Dust the wings with confectioner's sugar. Fill the bottom of the body with the chantilly cream. Place the head and wings and serve on a mirror of sauce. Garnish with raspberries and mint.

MEXICO

Journal – Mexico

Sail from Los Angeles

We are going home to Mexico. After all, the City of Angels originally belonged to the great Aztec family. The ship glides downwind through San Pedro's gusty Hurricane Gulch, past Angel's Gate and into the open sea. As the ship settles on an arcing southward course, the passengers drift away from the rails toward cocktails and dinner.

Port of call, Cabo San Lucas

The ship draws close to the brown-red rocky desert of Baja, banded with brilliant blue water. Getting closer, the color of the pyramided cape (cabo) startles into reds, oranges, yellows and ochres.

The afternoon is spent wandering among the sportfishing boats and pangas coming in with water-gushing catch tanks filled with sailfish, marlin, dorado and wahoo. Going to be a lot of good seafood barbecues tonight.

Near sun-down, the ship sails toward its own evening festivities. The tequila-giving agave plants shimmer among the paloverde and ocotillo trees on the gently sloping bajadas all the way to the heel of Baja's peninsula. After that, the ship pulls away from land, an amber-rayed sunset over her shoulder.

Port of call, Mazatlan

Over night, the ship has skirted the Sea of Cortez – she approaches Mazatlan, passing the backsides of three smallish islands before entering the port.

Before losing nerve, a parasailing boat is found and the harness strapped on. The signal is given and the speedboat roars out to sea, pulling the passenger into the sky. It's a terrifying moment – flying is, after all, an unnatural act for humans. Then,

SOUTHWESTERN DINNER

APPETIZERS

Brie and Papaya Quesadilla
Paysenne Peppers, Cilantro Sauce

Texas Lobster and Black Bean Soup
Lime-Marinated Lobster,
Crisp Corn Tortilla

Original Caesar Salad
Parmesan, Garlic, Croutons and Anchovy

ENTRÉES

Chili and Cumin-Rubbed Catfish
Charred Corn Relish, Steamed Okra and Fried Onions

Tequila Prawns
Flamed with Mexican Tequila and Serrano Chiles over Dirty Rice

Dry-Aged Filet Steak
Dried Pepper and Whiskey Marinade, Hominy and Cheddar Pudding

DESSERTS

Santa Fe Margarita
Lime, White Chocolate and Tequila

Canela Tortilla Stack
Pineapple, Rum, Raisins and Cinnamon Sugar

after just a few breaths, relaxation and enjoyment. The view is spectacular and it's so quiet. The landing on the beach is surprisingly soft. A definite do-again activity.

On the way back, a stop at a family-run cenaduria to nibble on chrorriadas (meaning "dirty faces" – fried gordita shells filled with pork, cheese, salsa, and beans, and fresh radishes) and Horchata (a very refreshing drink made with rice, sugar and cinnamon).

DAY 5 *Port of call, Puerto Vallarta*

The sun is just up over Punta de Mita, standing guard at the north end of the Bahia de Banderas with Puerto Vallarta in the crook of its arm. The ship ambles in to the Terminal Maritima and nobody rushes off to go sightseeing or beach hunting or shopping. Instead, passengers take their time, relaxing and easing their way into the day. The cruise must be working.

DAY 6 *Port of call, Zihuatanejo*

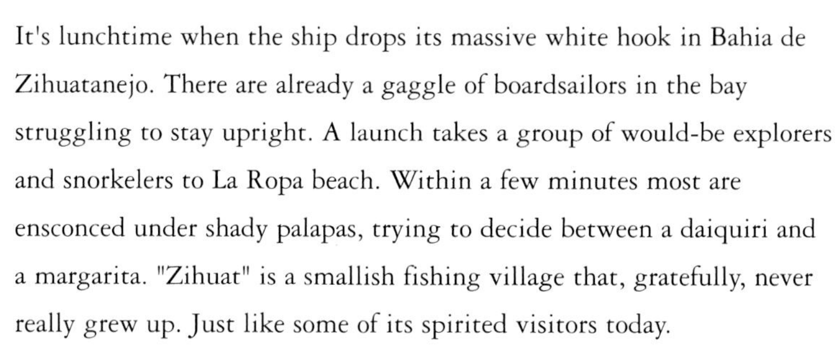

It's lunchtime when the ship drops its massive white hook in Bahia de Zihuatanejo. There are already a gaggle of boardsailors in the bay struggling to stay upright. A launch takes a group of would-be explorers and snorkelers to La Ropa beach. Within a few minutes most are ensconced under shady palapas, trying to decide between a daiquiri and a margarita. "Zihuat" is a smallish fishing village that, gratefully, never really grew up. Just like some of its spirited visitors today.

DAY 7 *Port of call, Acapulco*

Denial is heavy in many passenger's hearts this morning, as we come around the Isla Roqueta into Bahia de Acapulco. Today is the last day of the cruise (who makes these rules?). It's safe to say that no one wants this party to end. Yet, the day stretches out languorously and no one rushes. Today, is to be a day of pure spontaneity, save one sort-of plan to watch the famous Quedbrada cliff divers give new meaning to the phrase "no fear."

Although ashore there is nightlife galore, the ship's own celebrating community of friends and family is the best party around. New friends dance the night away, ready to keep the dawn from coming and the party to end. And like all such family gatherings, this nation-extended reunion with Mexico is really a beginning. For we will be back.

GARDE MANGER:

A DEDICATED AREA OF

THE GALLEY IN WHICH

COLD FOOD IS

PREPARED, SUCH AS

SHRIMP COCKTAIL,

FRESH SALADS

AND FRUIT CARVINGS.

BRIE AND PAPAYA QUESADILLA

Paysenne Peppers, Cilantro Sauce

Serves 6

6, 12-inch flour tortillas

2 tablespoons butter

FILLING

1 3/4 cups Brie cheese, small cubes

3/4 cup papaya, diced

1 to 2 jalapeños, chopped

2 teaspoons cilantro, chopped

1 tablespoon olive oil

salt and pepper

CILANTRO SAUCE

1/2 cup olive oil

1/4 cup corn oil

1/3 cup white wine vinegar

juice from 1 lime

2 teaspoons tequila

1 teaspoon jalapeño, chopped

2 tablespoons cilantro, chopped

1 tablespoon parsley, chopped

salt and pepper

1 red bell pepper

1 yellow bell pepper

1 green bell pepper

The tortilla is a staple bread in Latin American, Spanish and Southwestern cuisines. The dough is either made from wheat or corn flour, which is unleavened and becomes slightly tough after cooking. Although tortillas can be rolled or tossed into shape, they are traditionally formed using a specially designed tortilla press. This very versatile bread can be eaten on its own or used to complete a wide range of dishes from tacos to soup and even dessert. Tortillas can be baked, grilled over an open flame, fried on a griddle or deep-fried in oil.

Mix the ingredients for the filling of the tortillas together.

Melt the butter a little at a time as needed in a heavy sauté pan. Brown the tortillas lightly on both sides. Fill the tortillas with the mixture, fold in half like a turnover and return to the sauté pan. Cook over moderate heat, turning occasionally, until browned evenly and the cheese has melted.

Combine all of the ingredients for the sauce together and adjust the seasoning.

Trim and remove the seeds from the bell peppers and cut into small paysenne (diamond) shapes. Toss lightly with a little of the sauce and season.

Cut each quesadilla into thirds and serve with the paysenne peppers and the sauce.

The papaya garnish is made by cutting the stem end of a small papaya into a star shape and filling it with papaya seeds.

TEXAS LOBSTER AND BLACK BEAN SOUP

Lime-Marinated Lobster, Crisp Corn Tortilla

Serves 8 to 10

2 cups black beans, dried

1 smoked ham hock

2 bay leaves

8 cups water, chicken or lobster stock (p. 221)

3 cups lobster meat, large chunks

juice from 4 limes

2 tablespoons tequila

3 tablespoons olive oil

$1\frac{1}{2}$ cups onion, diced

6 cloves garlic, chopped

$\frac{1}{2}$ cup celery, diced

$\frac{3}{4}$ cup red pepper, diced

$\frac{1}{4}$ cup yellow pepper, diced

$\frac{1}{4}$ cup orange pepper, diced

2 jalapeños, chopped

$\frac{1}{2}$ teaspoon cayenne pepper

1 teaspoon coriander, ground

salt and pepper

4, 6-inch corn tortillas

fresh cilantro

Black beans are a common addition to Southwestern cooking in many forms and are exceptionally popular for use in soups. Their dark black skin helps to create a dramatic presentation while their creamy white flesh completes a mild-flavored and nutrient-rich composition. All dried beans should be soaked in cold water for 8 hours to overnight. When cooking, beans should be placed into cold water or stock and brought up to temperature slowly. This allows the starch to soften and absorb the liquid more easily. If you are cooking beans in advance, allow them to cool in their cooking liquid. Remember to taste and season the beans often.

Soak the black beans for 6 to 8 hours in cold lightly salted water. Drain and rinse well. Place the beans in a large soup pot with the ham hock, bay leaves and cold stock/water. Simmer gently uncovered for approximately 2 hours or until the beans are tender. Remove the grey foam that comes to the surface as the beans cook. Remove the ham hock and bay leaves from the soup. Using a stick mixer, processor or blender, blend half of the beans and liquid to a puree. Add the two back together to form a partially blended and thickened soup. Season.

Place the lobster meat in a bowl and add the lime juice and tequila. Marinate for 1 hour.

Heat the olive oil in a sauté pan. Sauté the onion and garlic until tender. Add the celery and the peppers and sauté 4 minutes more. Add the lobster and marinade and cook for 3 minutes. Add the remainder of the ingredients, combine well and season. Add the lobster mixture to the bean soup and simmer gently for 20 minutes. Adjust the seasoning before serving.

Meanwhile, preheat the oven to 350°F. Cut the tortilla into $\frac{1}{4}$-inch strips. Weave the strips together in a lattice pattern to approximately $2\frac{1}{2}$ inches square. Place the squares on a baking tray and bake until dried and golden brown, approximately 12 minutes. Season lightly with salt.

Serve the soup in large bowls and garnish with some of the lobster meat, peppers, crisp tortilla and fresh cilantro leaves.

ORIGINAL CAESAR SALAD

Parmesan, Garlic, Croutons and Anchovy

Serves 6

2 large heads romaine lettuce, hand leafed

2 cloves garlic

3 anchovy filets

1 egg, coddled

1½ teaspoons Dijon mustard

dash Worcestershire sauce

½ cup extra virgin olive oil

1½ tablespoons white wine vinegar

juice from 1 lemon

3 tablespoons Parmesan cheese, grated

salt and pepper

1 loaf French baguette

olive oil for sautéing

salt and pepper

6 ounces Parmesan cheese, shaved

12 anchovy filets

Coddling allows for the use of raw eggs in a dressing or emulsion while reducing the presence of bacteria through the application of heat without cooking the egg. Coddling is a cooking method that can also be used for preparing delicate fish and vegetables or for the gentle warming of already cooked foodstuffs. The idea is to gently heat the product by use of a water bath with either direct or indirect contact with the water.

Wash the romaine lettuce and drain in a cloth.

Bring 3 cups of water to a boil, reduce to a simmer and drop in the egg for exactly 1 minute. Remove from the water and let cool.

In a large bowl, preferably wooden, crush the garlic cloves and anchovy together with a pinch of salt. Add the coddled egg and mustard and combine well. Add the Worcestershire and drizzle in the olive oil to form an emulsion. Add the remainder of the ingredients, continuing to form an emulsion and adjust the seasoning. Toss the romaine leaves generously in the dressing.

Slice the baguette into ¼-inch thick slices. Heat the oil in a sauté pan and gently sauté the bread until well browned on both sides. Season.

Serve the leaves arranged nicely on a large plate and garnish with the croutons, anchovy filets and shaved Parmesan cheese. Finish with a sprinkle of fresh cracked black pepper.

CHILI AND CUMIN-RUBBED CATFISH

Charred Corn Relish, Steamed Okra and Fried Onions

Serves 6

12 small catfish filet portions, skin off, approximately 2 pounds

juice from 1 lemon

paprika, cumin and cayenne

oil for frying

CORN RELISH

1½ cups fresh corn

⅔ cup red pepper, diced

1 teaspoon garlic, chopped

¼ cup red onion, diced

¾ cup black beans, cooked

1 tablespoon red jalapeño, chopped

½ cup olive oil

juice from 1 lime

juice from 2 lemons

2 tablespoons cilantro, chopped

2 teaspoons parsley, chopped

salt and pepper

SEASONED FLOUR

1 cup flour

2 tablespoons salt

1 teaspoon white pepper

2 teaspoons paprika

1 tablespoon cumin

½ teaspoon cayenne pepper

1 large onion, thinly sliced

seasoned flour

oil for frying

salt and pepper

3 cups young okra

2 teaspoons butter

salt and pepper

Fresh okra is an un-ripened tropical plant. It originated in Africa and spread through the Americas, Asia and Europe although it is far less popular in the central and northern states than in the South. It is suitable for many cooking methods but is best when stewed which allows its fibrous exterior to break down and a stodgy liquid to form which aids in thickening. Its acidic flavor is an acquired taste but is essential for the making of specialty dishes such as Caribbean gumbo and Middle Eastern tajines.

Squeeze the lemon juice over the catfish filets. Season with the paprika, cumin and cayenne and dredge in seasoned flour. Heat enough oil in a heavy sauté pan to cover the bottom by ¼-inch. Shallow fry the catfish filets until golden and tender, approximately 6 minutes. Season and drain on absorbent paper.

Heat a heavy pan until very hot with no oil. Add the corn kernels to the hot pan and allow the kernels to char. Add the red peppers and cook, stirring for 5 minutes. Reduce the heat and add the garlic and onions. Cook 2 minutes just to combine the flavors, but not to soften the vegetables. Add the remainder of the ingredients, adjust the seasoning and keep warm.

Slice the onions very thin. Separate the rings and dust with seasoned flour. Quickly deep fry the onions until lightly browned. Season and drain on absorbent paper. The onions will darken slightly after they are removed from the oil. Season and keep warm.

Clean the okra and trim the stems. Steam the okra for 8 minutes whole. Once steamed, cut into ½-inch chunks if desired. Toss with butter, salt and pepper. Leaving the okra whole will help to contain the sap. It can also be cut and stewed if you prefer the natural characteristics of cooked okra.

Serve the fried fish with a generous amount of the corn relish, okra and fried onions.

TEQUILA PRAWNS

Flamed with Mexican Tequila and Serrano Chiles over Dirty Rice

Serves 6

36 jumbo tiger prawns

3 tablespoons olive oil

2 tablespoons serrano chiles, chopped

2 teaspoons garlic, chopped

½ cup white wine

¼ cup tequila

1 cup tomato concassé

¾ cup lime segments

¼ cup cream

1 tablespoon butter

3 tablespoons cilantro, chopped

salt and pepper

RICE

1 tablespoon butter

¼ cup onion, chopped

1 cup split grain rice

3 cups water, chicken or fish stock (p. 221)

½ cup tomato concassé

¼ teaspoon turmeric

½ teaspoon cumin

½ bay leaf

¼ cup cilantro leaves, rough cut

salt and pepper

12 green patty pans

1 teaspoon butter

salt and pepper

fresh cilantro

Tequila gets its name from its origin in Tequila, Mexico. Made from the fermented and distilled sap of the blue agave, it has a uniquely pungent flavor that varies greatly by producer due to the addition of colors, flavorings and natural aging. Many of the misconceptions about tequila qualities are due to marketing hype in labeling. The best tequilas have been aged for up to 3 years in oak. Tequila is a popular addition to recipes as its predominant flavor lends itself well to seafood and poultry. When purchasing good quality tequila, look for a high percentage value, 100% is best, of blue agave listed on the label as imitation tequilas are produced primarily of sugar cane and have been artificially flavored.

Peel and de-vein the prawns. Heat the olive oil in a large sauté pan and sauté the prawns for 2 minutes, turning them over once. Add the chiles and garlic and sauté 2 minutes more. Add the white wine and reduce until dry. Add the tequila and reduce, being careful as it may flame. Add the concassé and lime segments and toss together. Add the cream and cook 3 minutes allowing the tomatoes, lime juice and cream to form a light sauce. Stir in the butter and the cilantro and adjust the seasoning.

Meanwhile, melt the butter in a saucepan. Sauté the onions until soft. Add the rice and sauté for 3 or 4 minutes. Add the stock or water. Place the remainder of the ingredients into the pan, letting them settle on top of the rice, do not stir. Reduce the heat, cover the pan and cook for approximately 15 minutes. The rice should be soft and moist when cooked. Remove the bay leaf and adjust the seasoning before serving.

Sauté the patty pans whole or cut into quarters in the butter until just tender, approximately 4 minutes and season.

Arrange the prawns neatly on a bed of rice and top with the sauce of lime segments and tomato concassé. Serve with the sautéed patty pans and fresh cilantro leaves.

DRY-AGED FILET STEAK

Dried Pepper and Whiskey Marinade, Hominy and Cheddar Pudding

Serves 6

6, 8-ounce filet steaks

1 cup dried red chiles

12 garlic cloves

1/2 cup olive oil

2/3 cup whiskey

1 cherimoya, wedged

SAUCE

3/4 cup whiskey

3/4 cup white wine

1/2 teaspoon paprika

1 1/2 cups demi-glace (p. 220)

salt and pepper

CORN PUDDING

1 1/4 cups fresh corn kernels

3/4 cup hominy

1/3 cup onion, diced

1 teaspoon garlic, chopped

1 1/2 cups cream

1 tablespoon butter

3 tablespoons cornmeal

2/3 cup cheddar cheese, shredded

2 egg yolks

2 egg whites

nutmeg, salt and pepper

1/2 cup hominy kernels

2 large sweet potatoes

1/3 cup honey

3 tablespoons whiskey

Hominy is white or yellow corn, which has been dried, and removed of its shell and germ. This process can be done mechanically, but is often done chemically which helps to give the hominy part of its distinct flavor. It can be found dried, canned or frozen and is commonly served as a side dish or part of a casserole. Dried hominy can also be ground into grits, which makes a popular porridge.

Combine the first six ingredients together and marinate for 6 hours. Preheat a grill. Remove the filet from the marinade, season with salt and pepper and grill for approximately 9 minutes, turning regularly, for rare beef.

Place the wedges of cherimoya on the grill and cook for 2 minutes on each side.

Remove the dried chiles and garlic cloves from the remaining marinade and place in a saucepan. Add the whiskey and white wine and reduce by half. Add the paprika and demi-glace and simmer for 15 minutes until it coats a spoon. Adjust the seasoning and strain, reserving the chiles and garlic cloves.

Meanwhile, prepare the pudding. Preheat the oven to 350°F and butter 6, 6-ounce oven proof ramekins or molds. On the stove top, combine the first 8 ingredients for the pudding together in a saucepan and bring to a boil. Reduce to a simmer and cook for 10 minutes. The mixture should be the consistency of cottage cheese and may need a little more cream added depending on the moisture of the corn.

Let the mixture cool to room temperature. Stir in the egg yolks. Whisk the egg whites to a medium peak and fold into the mixture and season. Place a few kernels of hominy in the bottom of the ramekins. Fill the ramekins with the corn mixture. Place the ramekins on a tray and bake in the oven for 20 minutes or until the pudding has set.

Wash the sweet potatoes and place them in the oven to bake until they are just tender, 55 to 65 minutes. Remove from the oven and let cool slightly. Cut the potatoes into 3-inch sections and then into wedges. Combine the honey and whiskey together and brush it onto the wedges. Return the potatoes to the oven and bake 10 minutes longer. Season lightly with salt and pepper.

When serving, turn the pudding out onto the plates. The bottom may have to be trimmed if they do not stand up. Serve with the grilled filet, sweet potato, cherimoya wedges and sauce. Top the filet with dried chiles and garlic from the sauce.

SANTA FE MARGARITA

Lime, White Chocolate and Tequila

Serves 6

MOUSSE

2 cups heavy cream

6 ounces white chocolate

5 egg yolks

¼ cup sugar

¼ cup lime juice

2 tablespoons tequila

1 cup heavy cream

green food coloring

TUILES

½ cup unsalted butter

½ cup confectioner's sugar

1 teaspoon vanilla essence

½ cup flour

3 egg whites

confectioner's sugar for dusting

lime segments and zest

White chocolate, a wonderful invention, is not really chocolate at all. It is a combination of milk solids, cocoa butter, lecithin, sugar and flavorings, which is why it has no chocolate taste. White chocolate can be used in similar preparations as real chocolate, although it is slightly more temperamental when melting and is not as firm when set.

Bring the cream to a boil, reduce to a simmer and stir in the white chocolate until it has melted. Whisk the egg yolks and sugar together well until the eggs have become lightly frothy and the sugar dissolved. Whisk the cream and chocolate into the eggs and return to the stove. Add the lime juice and tequila and cook over moderate heat, stirring continuously, until the mixture thickens to coat the spoon well. Do not boil. Cool to room temperature.

Whisk the remaining cream to a stiff peak. If you would like to color the mousse slightly green, the best way is to put the coloring in the cream before whipping. This will help ensure even distribution of the color. Be careful when adding the color, you can always add more if necessary, but too much becomes unappetizing. Carefully fold the whipped cream into the white chocolate mixture. Cover the mousse with plastic wrap and refrigerate.

For the tuiles, cream the butter, vanilla and sugar together. Whisk the egg whites to a stiff peak. Fold the flour into the butter until smooth and then fold in the egg whites. Chill for 2 hours. Preheat the oven to 400°F.

Use a ⅛-inch thick piece of plastic, like the lid from a margarine container, and cut a flower shape out of it around 8 inches in diameter. Use this as a template and spread a thin layer of the tuile batter into it on a buttered baking sheet. Lift away the template and repeat the process. It is always a good idea to make a few more tuiles than you need as they are easy to break. Bake approximately 4 minutes or until the tuiles just start to turn brown. They will continue to brown as they set. The tuiles can be shaped while still warm by laying them into a small bowl so that the petals of the flower hang over the rim. Dust with confectioner's sugar when cool.

Spoon or pipe the mousse into the tuile bowls and garnish with lime segments or zest.

RAISINS

CANELA TORTILLA STACK

Pineapple, Rum, Raisins and Cinnamon Sugar

Serves 6

5, 6-inch flour tortillas

2/3 cup sugar

2 teaspoons cinnamon

1/2 cup butter, melted

3 cups fresh pineapple

3 tablespoons butter

1 cup pineapple juice

1/2 cup brown sugar

1/2 cup cream

2 tablespoons rum

2/3 cup raisins

1 cactus pear, wedged

cinnamon sticks

pineapple leaves

Cinnamon, most commonly thought of as a flavoring for desserts, has many other applications. Some cinnamon varieties can be almost hot and spicy in flavor, making them unusual additions to savory meat dishes and stews. Past cultures used cinnamon to flavor wine and yogurt drinks, as perfume and as an aphrodisiac. Although it stands well on its own, cinnamon is also good for mixing with other spices such as nutmeg, cayenne and cardamom.

Preheat the oven to 350°F. Cut the tortillas into quarters and lay onto baking trays. Mix the sugar and cinnamon together. Adjust cinnamon to desired flavor, using more or less as needed. Brush the tortillas generously with melted butter and then sprinkle with the cinnamon sugar. Bake the tortilla in the oven until golden brown, 6 to 8 minutes.

Peel and core the fresh pineapple. Cut into 1/4-inch thick slices and then cut the slices into halves. Melt the butter over high heat and then sauté the pineapple to just soften and take on a little color. Remove the pineapple and add the pineapple juice and brown sugar to the pan. Cook over high heat, stirring continuously, until the sugar begins to caramelize. Add the cream and rum to the sugar and stir continuously until the sauce becomes smooth and thickens slightly. Strain the sauce and then add the raisins while still hot. Let the sauce cool so that it is no longer steaming.

Serve the dessert by stacking layers of the pineapple and tortilla. Place the sauce around and dust with more cinnamon sugar. Garnish the plates with a rustic combination of the cactus pear, cinnamon stick and pineapple leaves.

FAR EAST

Journal – Far East

DAY 6,7 *Port of call, Shanghai, China*

The ship has traveled for a day across the East China Sea to reach Shanghai. We wander the day through gardens and parks, looking for connections between contemporary Chinese life and what remains of the several thousand year dynastic traditions, including the Yuyuan Gardens & Bazaar, built over an 18 year period by a wealthy Ming Dynasty official's family in 1559.

The food from informal street stalls (like New York hot dog stands) is the find of the day. Guotie or fried jiaozi are pot stickers like we've never tasted before – soft outside and crunchy inside with vegetables, pork or shrimp. We come back to the Yunnan Road Night Market to check out the enormous variety of produce, along with the caged ducks and chickens, and to taste more Shanghai "hot dogs."

DAY 13 *Port of call, Ho Chi Minh City, Vietnam (Phuy My)*

The ship ambles down the coast of Vietnam, soaking up its rural and dreamy atmosphere. Beautiful green fields and elegantly curved rice paddies. And crumbling French colonial buildings.

We've arrived in time to catch the Mid-Autumn Festival. This welcome-the-moon fête is especially appreciated by the children, who are given toys, cakes and fruit. Everywhere, with the full moon over their shoulder, food sellers offer us banh do (rice dumplings) and banh nuong (sweet cakes) in the shape of the moon and fish.

DAY 15 *Port of call, Singapore*

We're almost on the equator, it feels like we're at the sun's front gate. Not quite dressed in formal whites, we tour the colonial district. Then we take a rickshaw-like bicycle cart to Little India to shop for fabrics, curry spices and the ubiquitous, squiggly deep-fried chapatis. We also check out the mix of Malay and Chinese cooking, called Nonya – the coconut and lemon-grass-based soup, laksa, is the perfect antidote to the steamy heat of the equatorial sun.

LANDFALL DINNER

APPETIZERS

Premium Seafood and Avocado
Lemon-Lime Rémoulade

Vol-au-Vent à la Reine
Morel, Chicken and Sauteéd Sweetbreads

Double Beef Consommé
Oriental Dumpling and Alfalfa Sprouts

ENTRÉES

Asiago Cheese Stuffed Gnocchi
Fried Sage and Hazelnuts

Roasted Young Tom Turkey
Bread-Fruit Stuffing
and Glazed Sweet Potatoes

Old-Fashioned Pot-Roast Buffalo
Roasted Baby Root Vegetables,
Napa Valley Red Wine Sauce

Beef Wellington
Duchesse Potatoes, Sauce Bordelaise

DESSERTS

Grape Mille-Feuille
Soft Meringue, Poached Grapes,
Pinot Noir Sauce

Opera Cake
Almond Sponge, Kahlúa Cream
and White Chocolate Mousse

CHERVIL

PREMIUM SEAFOOD AND AVOCADO

Lemon-Lime Rémoulade

Serves 6

12 bay scallops

6 green shell mussels, shelled

1½ cups crab leg meat

12 jumbo tiger prawns, peeled and de-veined

RÉMOULADE

1 cup mayonnaise

1½ teaspoons mustard

1 teaspoon capers, chopped fine

1½ teaspoons gherkins, chopped fine

zest and juice from 1 lime

zest and juice from 2 lemons

2 teaspoons chervil, chopped

salt and white pepper

½ cup broccoli florets

3 large avocados

juice from 2 lemons

salt and pepper

zest from 1 lemon, julienne

zest from 1 lime, julienne

1 cup alfalfa sprouts

Avocados, primarily grown in California, can be as small as 1 ounce or as large as 4 pounds. The buttery flesh is most commonly eaten raw, but is also suitable for grilling due to its high fat content. Firm or unripened avocados can be placed into a paper bag or wrapped in newspaper to accelerate softening. The flesh will oxidize rapidly so either cut them just before serving or place them in acidulated water for a few minutes.

Combine all of the rémoulade ingredients well and adjust the seasoning. Prepare at least 30 minutes before serving to allow the flavors to develop.

Wash the seafood and steam 4 to 6 minutes for the scallops, mussels and crab, and 6 to 8 minutes for the prawns. Toss the warm seafood with a couple of tablespoons of the rémoulade. Place the seafood in the refrigerator to chill.

Steam the broccoli florets separately for 1 minute and chill.

Cut the avocados in halves and remove the seeds. Season the insides with salt and pepper and squeeze the lemon juice over them.

Arrange the seafood and broccoli in the avocado. Garnish with the julienne of zest and alfalfa sprouts. Serve the remaining rémoulade on the side.

VOL-AU-VENT À LA REINE

Morel, Chicken and Sautéed Sweetbreads

Serves 6

2 frozen puff pastry sheets
(sheets can be purchased in the freezer section of your local supermarket and are usually 1-foot x 1-foot square)

1 whole egg

1 pound sweetbread

2 cups milk

2 bay leaves

6 white peppercorns

flour for dusting

1 egg, beaten

1 cup brioche or white bread crumbs

RAGOÛT

1 tablespoon butter

½ cup onion, chopped

1 tablespoon garlic, chopped

3 cups chicken thigh meat, cubed

sweetbread cubes from above

1 cup morel mushrooms, chopped

½ cup white wine

2⅔ cups heavy cream

2 teaspoons fresh thyme, chopped

salt and pepper

2 tablespoons butter

1 pound spinach leaves

¼ cup white wine

salt and pepper

fresh thyme sprigs

Sweetbreads are the thymus glands and pancreas of lamb, pig and calves. The glands from the lamb and veal are preferred. The sweetbreads should always be soaked in brine or marinated in a milk solution until the blood has been drawn out. The thin membrane from around the glands should be peeled off; the sweetbread can be lightly poached to make this easier. Sweetbreads are delicate in flavor and suitable for any cooking method.

Preheat the oven to 425°F. Lay the puff pastry sheets out on the counter. Scramble the egg in a cup. Brush the puff pastry lightly and evenly with the egg. Using a 3-inch pastry cutter, cut 12 disks out of the puff pastry. Then use a 2 ½-inch cutter to cut the center out of 6 of the 3-inch disks, leaving 6 disks and 6 rings. Place one ring on top of each disk. Place the disks on a greased baking tray and bake for 12 to 15 minutes or until the pastry has risen and browned.

Place a piece of sweetbread in a bowl with the milk, bay leaves and peppercorns and marinate for 2 hours. Remove from the marinade and rinse with water. Peel any thick membrane or skin off of the sweetbread. Cut 6, ¼-inch slices off and cut the remainder into small cubes.

Season the slices lightly with salt and pepper. Dust with flour, dip in the egg and then coat with the bread crumbs. Sauté them for 3 minutes in butter just before serving. They should be golden brown and tender.

In a large saucepan, melt the butter and sauté the onions until tender. Add the garlic and cook 2 minutes more. Add the chicken and sweetbread cubes and sauté until both have turned opaque and are cooked halfway through. Add the mushrooms and white wine and cook until the wine has evaporated. Add the cream and herbs and simmer 7 to 10 minutes until the meat is tender and the sauce has thickened slightly. Adjust the seasoning.

Gently sauté the spinach leaves in the butter until the leaves begin to wilt, then add the white wine and allow to evaporate. Season the spinach well.

Place a vol-au-vent on each plate and fill with the ragoût. Garnish with sautéed spinach, a slice of sautéed sweetbread, more ragoût and fresh thyme.

DOUBLE BEEF CONSOMMÉ

Oriental Dumpling and Alfalfa Sprouts

Serves 6

12 cups beef stock (p. 220)

RAFT

3 egg whites
1 pound lean ground beef
1/2 onion, rough chopped
1 celery stalk, rough chopped
2 leeks, rough chopped
1 carrot, rough chopped
1 tomato, rough chopped
8 black peppercorns
1 bay leaf
2 garlic cloves

1/4 cup dry sherry
salt and pepper

WON TONS

12 won ton wrappers
1/2 pound ground pork
1/4 cup carrots, chopped
1/4 cup onion, chopped
1/4 cup cabbage, chopped
1 teaspoon garlic, chopped
1/2 teaspoon ginger, chopped
2 tablespoons soy sauce
1 1/2 teaspoons fresh chile, chopped
salt and pepper

CHOPSTICKS

1/2 cup enoki mushrooms
1/4 cup spring onion, chopped
1 cup alfalfa sprouts

oil for deep frying
12 spring roll sheets
1 egg, beaten

Consommé refers to a clarified stock. Classically made from beef, poultry or fish, modern cooking has popularized game, vegetable and even fruit consommés. Ironically, once you have mastered the skill of clarifying consommés, you may thicken them with cream or egg yolk as is sometimes done. Consommés can be served hot or cold and are generally garnished with any number of food items from vegetables and meats to profiteroles and custards.

The stock must be prepared in advance and chilled well. Combine all of the ingredients for the raft together. The vegetables should be washed before chopping, but do not have to be peeled. In a large stock pot, combine the cold stock and the raft together and mix well. The stock will now be cloudy and full of particles from the raft. Bring the stock to a simmer very slowly without stirring. All of the ingredients from the raft will begin to float to the surface and form a thick crust across the top of the stock. Simmer the stock gently for 45 minutes. The stock should simmer through the raft, but not boil. Add the sherry and some seasoning into the stock 10 minutes before the clarifying is done. Remove the pot from the heat and let sit for 15 minutes. Carefully remove a small piece of the raft. Ladle the stock out of the pot and strain through cheese cloth. The stock should be rich in color but very clear.

Combine all ingredients for the won tons, except the wrappers, in a food processor and mince together to form a rough textured paste. Test the seasoning by cooking a small amount of the filling separately and tasting. Adjust the seasoning. Place 1 tablespoon of the filling in the center of a won ton wrapper. Brush the edges of the wrapper lightly with water. Fold the wrapper over like a small turnover. Poach the won tons for 3 minutes in the consommé. This can be done separately with a small amount of consommé so as not to make the whole batch cloudy again.

Heat the oil to fry the chopsticks. Roll the spring roll sheets up tightly to form chopstick like shapes and brush with egg. Deep fry until golden brown. Remove from the oil onto a paper towel and season.

Serve the soup with the won tons and garnish with the mushrooms, spring onion, fried chopsticks and alfalfa sprouts.

SAGE

ASIAGO CHEESE STUFFED GNOCCHI

Fried Sage and Hazelnuts

Serves 6

2 pounds potatoes
3 tablespoons butter
2 eggs
1 egg yolk
$^2/_3$ cup flour
$^2/_3$ cup Parmesan cheese, grated

1 pound Asiago cheese

2 tablespoons butter
2 tablespoons, shallots, minced
1 teaspoon garlic, chopped
1$^1/_2$ cups Porcini mushrooms, sliced
1 cup white wine
1 quart heavy cream
juice from 1 lemon
$^1/_2$ cup Asiago cheese, shredded
$^1/_2$ cup Parmesan cheese, grated
salt, white pepper and nutmeg

$^1/_4$ cup olive oil
1 garlic clove
1 cup sage leaves
salt

$^1/_3$ cup hazelnuts, chopped

Potato dumplings are hearty and satisfying and are versatile enough to be served as an appetizer, in soups, in place of a pasta course, as a main entrée and even as a dessert. They can be poached and paired with any variety of sauce, baked like a casserole or pudding, or fried in oil. Preparing classic gnocchi dough is a little time-consuming and requires a bit of practice to form consistent shapes. They can be made in advance and frozen. If using frozen gnocchi, do not defrost before cooking.

Boil the potatoes whole until just cooked through. Peel and put through a ricer while still hot. Add the butter and eggs to the riced potatoes and combine well. Cool the potatoes and then kneed in the flour and Parmesan cheese to form a dough.

Flour the work surface and roll the dough out into $^1/_2$-inch diameter sticks and then cut the sticks into 1-inch long pieces. Cut the Asiago cheese into $^1/_4$-inch square pieces and push a piece of cheese into the center of each gnocchi. Roll the gnocchi in the palm of your hand to shape like a small football. Dust your hands and the gnocchi with flour as needed.

Bring a large pot of salted water to a boil. Add the gnocchi to the pot and boil until all of the gnocchi float to the top, 4 to 6 minutes. Drain and add to the sauce.

Melt the butter in a saucepan and sauté the shallots and garlic gently until tender. Add the mushrooms and sauté for 5 minutes. Add the white wine and continue to cook until the liquid has evaporated. Add the cream and simmer until reduced by half. Add the lemon juice and both cheeses and stir until smooth. Add the seasoning and simmer 5 minutes more. Adjust the seasoning.

Heat the oil and garlic together. Once the garlic clove begins to fry, add the sage leaves in and fry quickly. Be careful as the sage leaves will splatter when added to the oil. The sage leaves are ready when the oil stops bubbling, indicating that the water is all out of the leaves. Drain on a paper towel and season with salt.

Serve the gnocchi and sauce in a pasta bowl and garnish generously with fried sage leaves and chopped hazelnuts.

ROASTED YOUNG TOM TURKEY

Bread-Fruit Stuffing and Glazed Sweet Potatoes

Serves 8 to 10

1, 16-pound tom turkey

1 onion

2 carrots

2 celery stalks

12 cloves fresh garlic

fresh sage

salt and pepper

STUFFING

2 strips bacon, chopped

1 cup onions, small dice

2/3 cup celery, small dice

1 teaspoon garlic, chopped

3/4 cup apple, peeled and diced

1/4 cup prunes, diced

1/4 cup fresh cranberries

1/8 teaspoon nutmeg

1/8 teaspoon cayenne pepper

3 tablespoons fresh sage, chopped

8 cups dry bread pieces (white, wheat, corn or any combination)

2 eggs, beaten

2 cups turkey or chicken stock (p. 221)

salt and pepper

sweet potatoes (p. 219)

creamed peas (p. 220)

giblet gravy (p. 219)

cranberry dressing (p. 219)

Although the traditional bread-stuffing recipe is passed on through the family, there are a number of ways to create interesting combinations. Use different bread varieties as the base, such as rye, pumpernickel, cornbread, oat or brioche, mixed with flavorful wheat or white bread. Common additions to the stuffing include oysters, sausage, rice or potatoes along with dried fruits, seeds and chopped nuts. Stuffing is traditionally cooked inside the bird, but should be prepared separately. If stuffing the cavity is preferred, heat the stuffing to 165°F before placing in the turkey.

Preheat the oven to 425°F. Wash the turkey and trim off any excess fat. Remove the wing tips and reserve together with the neck and giblets for the sauce. Season the cavity well with sage, salt and pepper. Rough cut the onion, carrots and celery, peels and all. Add the garlic cloves and stuff the cavity. Truss the turkey with butcher's string.

In a roasting pan, place the turkey, giblets and bones in the oven. After 15 minutes, reduce the temperature to 325°F and roast for approximately 1 1/2 hours longer until the turkey is cooked through. The turkey is cooked when the juices run clear from the thigh. The wing tips, neck and giblets can be removed from the pan as soon as they are well-browned, approximately 40 minutes.

Sauté the bacon until well-browned. Add the onions and sauté; do not pour off excess fat. Add the celery and garlic and sauté until just tender. Add the apples, prunes, cranberries and spices and cook for 3 minutes; remove from the heat. In a large bowl, combine all the stuffing ingredients. Add the stock a little at a time. You may need a little more or less depending on how dry the bread is. The stuffing should be well moistened, but not soupy. Fill a casserole dish with the stuffing and cover with aluminum foil. Place in the oven with the turkey for 1 hour. Remove the foil for the last 15 minutes to allow the stuffing to brown.

Carve the turkey across the breast and thigh being sure to offer white and dark meat on each plate. Arrange with the potatoes, peas, stuffing, cranberry and gravy, and garnish with fresh sage.

OLD-FASHIONED POT-ROAST BUFFALO

Roasted Baby Root Vegetables, Napa Valley Red Wine Sauce

Serves 6

1, 5-pound buffalo roast
(chuck, top or bottom round may be used; beef may also be substituted)

1 carrot, quartered into long strips

salt and pepper

3 tablespoons vegetable oil

flour for dusting

MIREPOIX

1 onion, rough cut

1 carrot, rough cut

1 celery stalk, rough cut

1½ cups red wine

2 cups beef stock (p. 220)

2 cloves garlic

1 bay leaf

6 black peppercorns

MATIGNON

1 tablespoon butter

½ cup onion, small dice

1 cup carrot, small dice

½ cup celery, small dice

½ cup leek, small dice

⅓ cup turnip, small dice

1 cup potatoes, small dice

2 tablespoons flour

½ teaspoon fresh thyme, chopped

salt and pepper

18 baby carrots, peeled

18 baby turnips, peeled

2 teaspoons olive oil

chopped parsley

salt and pepper

Mirepoix is a basic, rough-cut mixture of onion, carrot and celery (more onion than carrot, more carrot than celery) used to flavor sauces and stews or as a base on which to place roasts. It is considered a staple in classic cooking and is not served with or in the meal. Matignon is used in a similar fashion to mirepoix, however, it is cut into a small uniform dice as it is meant to be left in the sauce or stew and served as part of the meal.

Preheat the oven to 300°F. Wash and dry the roast. Lard the roast with the carrots by making 4 incisions with a thin knife and forcing the carrot sticks through the roast. Dredge the roast in the flour. Heat the oil in a large Dutch oven or casserole on the stove top and brown the roast well on all sides. Add the vegetables for the mirepoix and brown. Arrange the vegetables in the bottom of the casserole so that the roast sits on top of them. Add the red wine, stock, garlic, bay leaf and peppercorns and bring to a boil. Cover and place the casserole in the oven. The roast will take 3 to 4 hours to cook. Turn the roast every 30 minutes and add a little stock as needed. Once cooked, remove the roast and let rest. Skim the fat off of the liquid and strain.

Sauté the vegetables for the matignon in the butter until just tender. Dust with the flour and stir well. Add the liquid from the pot roast to finish the sauce. Simmer gently for 10 minutes or until the sauce has reached the desired consistency. Season.

Split the baby vegetables and toss with the oil, parsley, salt and pepper. Place in a separate pan in the oven with the roast for the last 25 minutes to cook.

Slice the roast and serve on a generous portion of the vegetables and sauce.

DUXELLES

BEEF WELLINGTON

Duchesse Potatoes, Sauce Bordelaise

Serves 6

1, 3-pound beef tenderloin, trimmed

oil for searing

salt and pepper

DUXELLES

1½ pounds button mushrooms

⅔ cup onion

3 cloves garlic

¾ cup bread crumbs

2 teaspoons fresh thyme, chopped

⅛ teaspoon cayenne pepper

¼ teaspoon nutmeg

salt and pepper

2 frozen puff pastry sheets
(sheets can be purchased in the freezer section of your local supermarket and are usually 1-foot x 1-foot square)

1 whole egg

BORDELAISE SAUCE

2 cups red wine

1 sprig fresh thyme

1 bay leaf

9 black peppercorns

¼ cup mushroom stems and pieces

4 cups demi-glace (p. 220)

duchesse potatoes (p. 171)

1 pound broccoli, florets

1 pound carrots, julienne

2 tablespoons butter

salt and pepper

Duxelles is a culinary term used to describe a combination of chopped mushrooms, onions, garlic and herbs, cooked together until most of the moisture has evaporated. This dark, thick mixture is used to stuff meats and vegetables, as a garnish in sauces or as an accompaniment to a main dish.

Season the tenderloin and sear in a very hot pan on all sides. Set aside.

Place all of the ingredients for the duxelles in a food processor and mince. Transfer the mix to a large sauté pan and cook over moderate heat until the majority of the water has evaporated so the duxelles is wet, but not runny. Season well.

Preheat the oven to 475°F. Lay the puff pastry sheets out on a floured surface putting the ends together to form one long sheet. Spread the duxelles over the pastry. Place the tenderloin in the center and roll it up so that the duxelles surrounds the tenderloin. Seal the edges well and place the Wellington on a greased baking tray. Scramble the egg and use a pastry brush to coat the Wellington evenly with the egg. Place the Wellington in the oven and bake for 40 minutes for medium rare. Remove the Wellington and let rest for 5 minutes before slicing.

Place the wine, thyme, bay leaf, peppercorns and mushrooms in a saucepan and bring to a boil. Simmer the liquid until it has reduced by half. Add the demi-glace and reduce by one-third or until the sauce will coat a spoon. Adjust the seasoning and strain the sauce.

Prepare the duchesse potatoes.

Steam the broccoli and carrots until just tender but still crisp and toss in the butter, salt and pepper.

Use a serrated bread knife to slice the Wellington. Serve with the vegetables, potatoes and bordelaise sauce.

GRAPE MILLE-FEUILLE

Soft Meringue, Poached Grapes, Pinot Noir Sauce

Serves 6

8 sheets phyllo dough

1/2 cup butter, melted

MERINGUE

2 cups sugar

1/4 teaspoon cream of tartar

1 cup water

6 egg whites

SAUCE

2 cups white seedless grapes

2 cups red seedless grapes

1 1/2 cups Pinot Noir

1/4 cup honey

1/4 cup sugar

1/3 cup apple juice

juice from 1 lemon

1/2 clove

confectioner's sugar for dusting

Meringue is an easy-to-prepare combination of egg whites and sugar that becomes a versatile addition to desserts and sweet snacks. The meringue can be cooked over a water bath, burnt with a torch or under a broiler, or baked until dry in the oven. It can be used as a topping or icing, as a filling or made into individual kisses, the name commonly given to bite size meringue confections.

Preheat the oven to 350°F. Working quickly to prevent the sheets from drying out, lay four sheets of phyllo pastry out on the counter. Gently brush each sheet with melted butter. Lay a second sheet on top of each of the first four and brush with butter again. Use a 4-inch cutter or a glass to cut 24 circles out of the sheets of pastry. Place the circles on a buttered baking tray and bake for 6 to 8 minutes or until golden brown. Be very careful when handling the pastry as it will brake easily. If a piece does break or chip, you can use it in the center of the mille-feuille.

In a saucepan, dissolve the sugar and cream of tartar in the water and bring to a boil. Cook covered until a temperature of 240°F is reached, remove from the heat and cool slightly. Meanwhile, whisk the egg whites to a soft peak. Continue to whisk and drizzle in the hot sugar syrup. Whisk the meringue until cool and a medium peak is achieved.

Cut the grapes in half and use a small knife to pull the peel off of them. This takes a bit of time, but the skin will come off quite easily after a little practice.

Place the wine, honey, sugar, apple juice, lemon juice and clove in a saucepan and bring to a boil. Reduce the heat and simmer gently until the liquid forms a light sauce. Taste the sauce often and remove the clove as soon as the desired flavor is achieved. Place the grapes in the sauce and poach for 3 to 4 minutes, just to soften the grapes then remove and cool. Do not leave the grapes in the sauce or the water will seep out of them and make the sauce too thin.

Assemble the mille-feuille by layering the grapes and meringue between the phyllo circles in a decorative pattern for a total of 4 layers of pastry. Garnish with a dusting of confectioner's sugar and drizzle the plate with the sauce. Serve at once or the pastry will begin to soften.

OPERA CAKE

Almond Sponge, Kahlúa Cream and White Chocolate Mousse

Ganache, a mixture of scalded fresh cream and melted chocolate, is a rich and delicious addition to cakes and pastries. It can be made with semi-sweet, dark or white chocolate and flavored with alcohol for variety. It can be poured over a cake and allowed to set to form a perfectly smooth coating, or it can be whipped to double its volume and used to ice cakes or fill pastries.

Serves 8 to 10

MOUSSE

2 cups heavy cream

6 ounces white chocolate

5 egg yolks

1/4 cup sugar

1/4 cup amaretto

Bring the cream to a boil, reduce to a simmer and stir in the white chocolate until it has melted. Whisk the egg yolks and sugar together well until the eggs have become lightly frothy and the sugar dissolved. Whisk the cream and chocolate into the eggs and return to the stove. Add the amaretto and cook over a moderate heat, stirring continuously, until the mixture thickens to coat the spoon well. Do not boil. Cool to room temperature.

1 cup heavy cream

Whisk the remaining cream to a stiff peak. Carefully fold the whipped cream into the white chocolate mixture. Cover the mousse with plastic wrap and refrigerate.

vanilla sponge (p. 150)

1/4 cup amaretto

1/3 cup Kahlúa

1/2 cup espresso coffee

2 tablespoons sugar

1/8 teaspoon cinnamon

Prepare the sponge in thin layers as described in the recipe. Cut the sheets into 5, 1-foot x 1-foot pieces. Place one piece of sponge on a baking tray or in a cake pan. Combine the amaretto, Kahlúa, espresso, sugar and cinnamon together and sprinkle the sponge generously with the mixture. Spread a thin layer of white chocolate mousse over the sponge. Place another piece of sponge over the mousse and repeat the process three more times ending with a layer of sponge on top. Refrigerate.

chocolate ganache (p. 218)

Prepare the chocolate ganache. Once cooled slightly, coat the top of the cake with the ganache. You may need to coat the cake more than once to achieve a consistent smooth surface. Allow to cool so the ganache will set.

chocolate sauce (p. 150)

amaretto sauce (p. 218)

KAHLÚA SAUCE
(Makes 4 cups)

6 each egg yolks

1/2 cup sugar

2 1/2 cups milk

3/4 cup Kahlúa

1/4 cup espresso coffee

1/4 cup brandy

To prepare the Kahlúa sauce, cream the egg yolks and sugar together gently without incorporating too much air. Meanwhile, split and scoop out the vanilla bean, add to the milk and bring just to a boil. Slowly add the hot milk into the eggs and sugar mixture until it is well combined. Return the mixture to a moderate heat. Add the Kahlúa, espresso and brandy and continue to cook until the sauce thickens and coats the back of a spoon. Do not boil the sauce or it will curdle. Remove from the heat and cool. Serve warm or cold.

Prepare the other two sauces and place them into separate squeeze bottles.

cocoa powder

Using a sharp knife, cut the cake into 8 equal pieces. Place the cake in the center of the plate. Use the squeeze bottles to place small dots of the sauce around the plate in an alternating pattern. Use a toothpick to draw a line through the sauces to create the heart shapes. Garnish with shavings of white chocolate and cocoa powder.

Mocha, Grand Marnier, Harlequin, French Vanilla,

Passion Fruit, Strawberry and Chocolate: in number and variety,

Princess Cruises offers more soufflés.

BASIC

BRIOCHE

Makes 1 loaf

6 tablespoons butter
2 cups flour
1 cake compressed yeast
2 tablespoons warm water

1 tablespoon sugar
1 teaspoon salt
2 eggs, room temperature
2 to 3 tablespoons milk

1 egg
¼ cup milk

Butter and flour a bread loaf pan.

Mix ½ cup of the flour together with the compressed yeast and water. Place this mixture in a covered bowl and put in a warm place, the dough should not be warmer than 85°F or the yeast will die. Let the dough rise until it has doubled in size.

Kneed the remainder of the flour with the sugar, salt, eggs and milk. This mixture will be slightly wet and should be worked forcefully for approximately 15 minutes to develop the gluten in the dough. Once the dough has come together to form a smooth shiny consistency, work in the soft, not melted, butter. Work together the two dough mixtures until you have one smooth ball of dough. Place the ball in a floured bowl, cover and refrigerate for 1 hour.

Preheat oven to 450°F.

Form the chilled dough into a log and place in the prepared bread pan. Put in a warm area and allow to rise until the loaf has doubled in size. Mix the egg and milk together and brush the top of the loaf with the egg wash. Bake for approximately 25 to 30 minutes or until a dark golden brown is achieved and the loaf has set. Remove from the oven and pan and cool on a rack.

COOKED RICH TOMATO SAUCE

Makes approximately 3 quarts of sauce

4 pounds Roma tomatoes, peeled, seeded and chopped
½ cup olive oil
2 cups onion, small dice
1 cup carrots, small dice
½ cup leeks, small dice
½ cup celery, small dice
⅔ cup tomato paste
½ cup flour
1 cup red wine
3 cups beef stock (p. 220)
(chicken stock, vegetable stock or water can be substituted)

2 teaspoons sugar
8 cloves fresh garlic, chopped
3 bay leaves

¼ cup fresh basil, chopped
¼ cup fresh oregano, chopped
salt and pepper

When in season, use fresh Roma tomatoes. Peel them by cutting a small X in the end of the tomato (opposite the stem end). Place the tomatoes in boiling water for approximately 20 seconds. Remove from the boiling water and place into ice water to stop them from cooking. The peel can then be pulled off with your hands or by using a small knife. Cut the tomatoes in half, remove and discard the seeds and the stem end and rough chop. Alternatively, use a good quality canned Roma tomato that has been peeled and seeded.

Heat half of the olive oil gently in a heavy stock pot. Sauté the onions, carrots, leeks and celery until translucent. Increase the heat; add the tomato paste and cook, stirring continuously until the paste browns. Add the flour and continue to cook and stir until it has browned. Add the red wine and allow to evaporate. Add the beef stock, tomatoes, sugar and garlic. Cook for approximately 30 minutes until everything is tender. Using a stick mixer or a food processor, remove from the heat and blend the sauce until smooth, being careful not to burn yourself. Return the sauce to the heat and add the bay leaves and the remaining olive oil; continue to cook for approximately 1½ hours more, stirring occasionally. 30 minutes before serving, add the fresh herbs and season with salt and pepper. The sauce should be rich, dark and slightly thickened.

HORSERADISH CREAM

Makes 2 cups

⅓ cup horseradish, grated
½ cup heavy cream, whipped
1½ cups sour cream
1 teaspoon mustard
1 dash Worcestershire sauce
1 dash Tabasco
juice from 1 lemon
2 teaspoons fresh parsley, chopped
salt and pepper

Peel and grate horseradish. Whisk the cream to a medium peak. Combine all ingredients together. Adjust seasoning again just before serving.

BÉCHAMEL SAUCE

Makes 1 quart

⅓ cup butter
⅓ cup flour

1 quart milk
1 small onion
3 cloves
1 bay leaf
nutmeg, salt and white pepper

Melt the butter in a saucepan, but do not brown. Stir in the flour to make a roux. Cook the roux over moderate heat for 5 minutes, stirring continuously. The roux should be stiff, but not dry and crumbly. Cool to room temperature. In a separate pan, bring the milk to a boil and reduce to a simmer. Whisk the roux into the hot milk. Stud the onion with the cloves and bay leaf and place in the sauce. Cook for at least 10 minutes. Season the sauce with the nutmeg, salt and pepper and then strain. The sauce can be thinned with more milk if necessary.

STRAWBERRY-COINTREAU ICE CREAM

Makes 3½ cups

1¾ cups fresh cream

¼ cup Cointreau

¾ cup strawberries, chopped

5 tablespoons sugar

5 egg yolks

Bring the cream and Cointreau just to the boiling point. Meanwhile, mix the sugar and egg yolks together to form a smooth paste. Slowly mix the milk into the paste mixture. Return the mixture to the stove over a double boiler. Do not boil again. Add the strawberries. Continue cooking until it has thickened enough to heavily coat the back of a spoon. Remove the mixture from the heat and stir over a water bath until chilled. Freeze in an ice cream machine.

FONDANT

Makes 4 cups

1 cup water

3 cups sugar

1/16 teaspoon cream of tartar

confectioner's sugar for dusting

Bring the water to a boil in a heavy saucepan. Remove from the heat and dissolve the sugar. Return to the heat and bring back to a light boil. Add the cream of tartar and stir vigorously. Cover the pan and cook for 3 minutes allowing the steam to wash down the sides of the pan. Uncover and continue to simmer the mixture without stirring until it has reached a soft-ball, 234°F. Pour the mixture onto a marble or granite slab and cool until the fondant begins to hold its own shape. Using a scraper or wooden spoon, work the fondant from the edges into the center until the mixture turns from translucent to opaque. Kneed the fondant by hand, dusting it with powdered sugar as necessary, until smooth. Wrap tightly with plastic wrap once cool and store in the pantry up to a week.

BUTTERMILK-VANILLA ICE CREAM

Makes 3½ cups

1½ cups fresh cream

1 cup buttermilk

1 vanilla bean

7 tablespoons sugar

5 egg yolks

Bring the cream, milk and vanilla bean just to the boiling point. Meanwhile, mix the sugar and egg yolks together to form a smooth paste. Remove the vanilla bean from the milk and slowly mix the milk into the paste mixture. Return the mixture to the stove over a double boiler. Do not boil again. Scrape the seeds from the vanilla bean and add to the mixture. Continue cooking until it has thickened enough to heavily coat the back of a spoon. Remove the mixture from the heat, strain through a fine sieve and stir over a water bath until chilled. Freeze in an ice cream machine.

CHOCOLATE-RUM ICE CREAM

Makes 3½ cups

1½ cups fresh cream

½ cup milk

6 ounces chocolate, chopped

3 tablespoons sugar

¼ cup dark rum

5 egg yolks

Bring the cream, milk and rum just to the boiling point. Meanwhile, mix the sugar and egg yolks together to form a smooth paste. Slowly mix the milk into the paste mixture. Return to the stove over a double boiler. Do not boil again. Add the chopped chocolate. Continue cooking until it has thickened enough to heavily coat the back of a spoon. Remove the mixture from the heat and strain through a fine sieve and stir over a water bath until chilled. Freeze in an ice cream machine.

CHOCOLATE GANACHE

Makes 4 cups

2½ cups semi-sweet chocolate

2 tablespoons butter

1¼ cups heavy cream

2 tablespoons brandy, optional

Chop the chocolate roughly and place in a large bowl with the butter. Bring the cream and brandy just to a boil. Remove from the heat and pour over the chopped chocolate. Stir together gently until the chocolate has completely melted. The mixture will thicken as it cools. For coating, use the ganache just above room temperature so it pours evenly, but not so hot that it is runny. For a mousse, cool the ganache to room temperature and then whip with a mixer until doubled in volume. Refrigerate unused ganache.

AMARETTO SAUCE

Makes 4 cups

6 egg yolks

½ cup sugar

2½ cups milk

½ vanilla bean

⅓ cup amaretto

¼ cup brandy

Cream the egg yolks and sugar together gently without incorporating too much air. Meanwhile, split and scoop out the vanilla bean, add to the milk and bring just to a boil. Slowly add the hot milk into the eggs and sugar mixture until well combined. Return the mixture to a moderate heat. Add the amaretto and brandy and continue to cook until the sauce thickens and coats the back of a spoon. Do not boil the sauce or it will curdle. Remove from the heat and cool. Serve warm or cold.

CRANBERRY DRESSING

Makes 1 quart

3 cups fresh cranberries

1 cup water

½ cup white wine

1¼ cups sugar

juice from 1 orange

2 tablespoons shallots, minced

¼ cup celery, finely chopped

¼ teaspoon dry mustard

¼ piece cinnamon stick

1 clove

salt and pepper

Place the cranberries, water, wine and sugar into a pan and bring to a boil. Reduce heat and simmer for 10 minutes. Add the remaining ingredients and simmer 10 minutes more. Remove the cinnamon and clove and adjust the seasoning. The sauce can be served chunky or pureed.

FIERY TOMATO SAUCE

Makes approximately 2 quarts of sauce

4 pounds Roma tomatoes, peeled, seeded and chopped

¼ cup olive oil

2 cups onion, small dice

10 cloves fresh garlic, chopped

¼ cup fresh chiles, chopped

1 teaspoon sugar

¼ cup fresh basil, chopped

¼ cup fresh oregano, chopped

2 teaspoons red chili flakes

salt and pepper

1 teaspoon butter, cold

When in season, use fresh Roma tomatoes. Peel them by cutting a small X in the end of the tomato (opposite the stem end). Place the tomatoes in boiling water for approximately 20 seconds. Remove from the boiling water and place into ice water to stop them from cooking. The peel can then be pulled off with your hands or by using a small knife. Cut the tomatoes in half, remove and discard the seeds and the stem end and rough chop. Alternatively, use a good quality canned Roma tomato that has been peeled and seeded.

Heat the olive oil gently in a heavy stock pot. Sauté the onions and garlic until translucent. Add the chiles and sauté 2 minutes. Increase the heat and add the chopped tomatoes and the sugar. If the tomatoes are very sweet, omit the sugar from the recipe. Stir the tomatoes often to allow for evaporation and prevent burning, approximately 10 minutes. Add the fresh herbs and dried chili and season with the salt and pepper. Cook 3 more minutes, stir in the cold butter and serve immediately.

LAMB JUS

Makes 1 quart

3 pounds lamb bones or meat scraps

1¼ cups mirepoix (p. 208)

6 cloves garlic

½ cup tomato paste

1 cup red wine

5 black peppercorns

3 bay leaves

1 clove

½ bunch fresh thyme

1 sprig rosemary

3 quarts water

salt and pepper

Preheat the oven to 425°F. Place the bones in a roasting pan and put in the oven to brown. The bones will require at least 30 minutes to brown, stir occasionally. Once well-browned, add the mirepoix and garlic and return to the oven to brown an additional 20 minutes, stirring occasionally. Add the tomato paste and stir well to distribute evenly. Return to the oven and brown for 10 minutes. Add the red wine and return to the oven, stirring occasionally until the wine has almost evaporated. Add the remaining ingredients and simmer gently in the oven for approximately 1 hour. Remove from the oven and remove the foam and fat that comes to the surface. The jus should be well reduced and should be rich in color and flavor. Strain and adjust the seasoning. This can be made in large batches then divided into small containers and stored in the freezer.

GLAZED SWEET POTATOES

Serves 6

3 to 4 large sweet potatoes

2 tablespoons butter

2 tablespoons brown sugar

1 tablespoon maple syrup

¼ teaspoon mustard powder

⅛ teaspoon cayenne pepper

⅛ teaspoon cinnamon

salt and pepper

Preheat the oven to 400°F. Wash the sweet potatoes and place on a baking tray. Do not prick or oil the potatoes. Bake for approximately 50 minutes or until just cooked, being careful not to over cook them. Cool.

Peel the cooled sweet potatoes and cut them into medium sized cubes.

In a large sauté pan, heat the butter and remaining ingredients together to form a light caramel. Add the potato cubes to the pan and brown together. Season and serve with a drizzle of the sauce.

GIBLET GRAVY

Makes 1 quart

⅓ cup butter

⅓ cup flour

1 quart turkey stock (p. 221)

¼ cup onion, diced

½ cup giblets, cooked and chopped

1 bay leaf

2 teaspoons fresh sage, chopped

nutmeg, salt and pepper

Melt the butter in a saucepan, but do not brown. Stir in the flour to make a roux. Cook the roux over moderate heat for 8 minutes, stirring continuously. The roux should be stiff, but not dry and crumbly and should be a light golden brown. Cool to room temperature. In a separate pan, bring the stock to a boil and reduce to a simmer. Whisk the roux into the stock. Cook for 10 minutes and then strain into another saucepan. Add the onion, giblets, sage and seasoning to the sauce and simmer gently for 10 minutes more. Pan juices can also be used for the liquid if you are roasting a turkey when making this sauce.

CREAMED PEAS

Serves 6

1½ pounds fresh or frozen peas

2 tablespoons shallots, minced
1 teaspoon garlic, minced
⅓ cup white wine
½ teaspoon mustard
1¼ cups cream
salt and pepper

fresh chopped mint, optional

Frozen peas need no preparation. Fresh peas should be blanched for 3 minutes in salted boiling water then strained. In a saucepan, sweat the shallots until soft. Add the garlic and sauté. Add the white wine and reduce to a syrup. Add the mustard and cream and simmer for 3 to 4 minutes. Add the peas and simmer a few minutes more to heat the peas thoroughly and slightly thicken the sauce. Season. Fresh mint can be added at the last minute.

DEMI-GLACE

Makes 1 gallon

½ cup vegetable oil
8 pounds beef bones
2 cups mirepoix (p. 208)
6 cloves garlic
1¼ cups tomato paste
½ cup flour
2 cups red wine
12 black peppercorns
3 bay leaves
1 bunch fresh thyme
2 gallons beef stock (p. 220)
(water may be substituted)
salt and pepper

Preheat the oven to 425°F. Place the oil and bones in a roasting pan and put in the oven to brown. The bones will require at least 30 minutes to brown; stir occasionally. Once well-browned, add the mirepoix and garlic and return to the oven to brown an additional 30 minutes, stirring occasionally. Add the tomato paste and stir well to distribute evenly. Return to the oven and brown for 15 minutes. Add the flour and stir well then add the red wine and return to the oven, stirring occasionally until a thick paste has formed around the bones and vegetables. Transfer everything from the roasting pan into a large stock pot. Add the remaining ingredients and simmer gently for at least 2 hours, up to 6. Regularly remove the foam and fat that comes to the surface. The sauce should reduce by approximately half and should be rich in color and flavor and should coat the back of a spoon. Strain the demi-glace and adjust the seasoning. This can be made in large batches then divided into small containers and stored in the freezer.

FISH STOCK

Makes 2 quarts

4 pounds fish bones and heads
1½ cups mirepoix (p. 208)
4 cloves garlic
¼ cup tomato, chopped
1 cup white wine
½ cup vermouth
6 white peppercorns
2 bay leaves
1 clove
2 sprigs fresh parsley
juice from 2 lemons
1 gallon water
salt and pepper

Wash the fish bones thoroughly. Place all of the ingredients in a large stock pot. Bring to a boil very slowly and then simmer gently for 45 minutes to 1 hour. Regularly remove the foam and fat that comes to the surface. The stock should reduce by half and be very light in color, but rich in flavor. Strain and adjust the seasoning.

LOBSTER STOCK

Makes 2 quarts

2 pounds lobster shells
2 pounds fish bones and heads
1½ cups mirepoix (p. 208)
4 cloves garlic
¼ cup tomato, chopped
1 cup white wine
½ cup vermouth
6 white peppercorns
2 bay leaves
1 clove
2 sprig fresh parsley
2 sprigs fresh tarragon
juice from 2 lemons
1 gallon water
salt and pepper

Follow the directions for the fish stock, above.

BEEF STOCK

Makes 1 gallon

5 pounds beef bones
3½ cups mirepoix (p. 208)
6 cloves garlic
1¼ cups tomato paste
2 cups red wine
10 black peppercorns
3 bay leaves
1 clove
1 bunch fresh thyme
2 gallons water
salt and pepper

Preheat the oven to 425°F. Place the bones in a roasting pan and put in the oven to brown. The bones will require at least 30 minutes to brown, stir occasionally. Once well browned, add the mirepoix and garlic and return to the oven to brown an additional 30 minutes, stirring occasionally. Add the tomato paste and stir well to distribute evenly. Return to the oven and brown for 15 minutes. Add the red wine and return to the oven, stirring occasionally until the wine has almost evaporated. Transfer everything from the roasting pan into a large stock pot. Add the remaining ingredients and simmer gently for at least 2 hours, up to 6. Regularly remove the foam and fat that comes to the surface. The stock should reduce by approximately half and should be rich in color and flavor.

Strain and adjust the seasoning. This can be made in large batches then divided into small containers and stored in the freezer.

VEAL STOCK

Makes 1 gallon

5 pounds veal bones
2½ cups mirepoix (p. 208)
6 cloves garlic
½ cups tomato paste
2 cups white wine
5 black peppercorns
5 white peppercorns
3 bay leaves
1 clove
½ bunch fresh thyme
2 gallons water
salt and pepper

Follow the directions for the beef stock, above.

CHICKEN STOCK

Makes 1 gallon

8 pounds chicken bones
3 cups mirepoix (p. 208)
6 cloves garlic
¼ cup tomato, chopped
1½ cups white wine
8 white peppercorns
3 bay leaves
1 clove
1 sprig fresh thyme
1 sprig fresh parsley
2 gallons water
salt and pepper

Wash the chicken bones thoroughly. Place all of the ingredients in a large stock pot. Bring to a boil very slowly and then simmer gently for 1½ to 2 hours. Regularly remove the foam and fat that comes to the surface. The stock should reduce by half and be light in color but rich in flavor. Strain and adjust the seasoning. For a brown stock, the chicken bones can be roasted in the oven first.

TURKEY STOCK

Makes 1 gallon

8 pounds turkey bones
3 cups mirepoix (p. 208)
6 cloves garlic
¼ cup tomato, chopped
1½ cups white wine
8 white peppercorns
3 bay leaves
1 clove
¼ cup juniper berries
1 sprig fresh thyme
1 sprig fresh parsley
2 gallons water
salt and pepper

Follow the directions for the chicken stock, above.

VEGETABLE STOCK

Makes 1 gallon

6 cups vegetables
(any assortment of vegetables and vegetable scraps can be used such as carrots, celery, onion, leek, cabbage, tomato, mushroom, etc.)
4 cloves garlic
2 bay leaves
1 clove
1 sprig fresh parsley
1 sprig fresh thyme
1 cup white wine
juice from 1 lemon
5 white peppercorns
salt and pepper
2 gallons water

Place all of the ingredients in a large stock pot. Bring to a boil slowly. Reduce to a simmer and cook gently for 45 minutes. Regularly remove the foam off of the surface. The stock should reduce by half. Strain and adjust the seasoning.

PÂTE BRISÉE

Makes one 9-inch crust

½ cup butter
3 tablespoons vegetable shortening
2 cups all-purpose flour
½ teaspoon of salt
5 to 6 tablespoons cold water

For the pastry, work the butter and shortening into the flour until crumbly. Add the water a little at a time until the dough gathers softly without sticking to your fingers. Wrap and refrigerate the dough for at least 2 hours, up to 36 hours.

CHIVE SAUCE

Serves 6

2 tablespoons shallots, minced
1 teaspoon garlic, minced
1 sprig of parsley
4 each white peppercorns
1½ cups white wine
juice from two lemons
1½ cups fish stock (p. 220)
(if not using fish stock, replace with more cream, not water)
2 cups heavy cream
¼ cup fresh chives, chopped
1 teaspoon butter
salt and white pepper

Combine the shallots, garlic, parsley, peppercorns, white wine and lemon juice in a saucepan and bring to a boil. Reduce the heat and simmer until the liquid has almost formed a syrup. Add the fish stock and reduce by half. Add the cream and reduce by half again or until the sauce has reached the desired consistency. Adjust the seasoning of the sauce and strain. Add the chopped chives and swirl in the butter just before serving.

INDEX

Barley, Chickpea and Dried Fruit, p.118

Beef
- Châteaubriand, p.170
- Dry-Aged Filet Steak, p.190
- Seared Tenderloin of Beef Carpaccio, p.68
- Slow-Roasted Prime Rib of Beef, p.20
- Wellington, p.210

Blini, p.156

Brioche, p.217

Carrots, Glazed, p.100

Caviar, A Symphony of, p.156

Celery à la Crème, p.170

Cheesecake, p.22

Chicken
- Breast of Chicken à la Kiev, p.78
- Conchiglie alla Campagnola, p.16
- Vol-au-Vent à la Reine, p.200
- Warm Grilled Chicken Supreme, p.48

Chocolate
- Chocolate Grand Marnier Cake, p.62
- Chocolate Sauce, p.150
- Chocolate-Mocha Sauce, p.174
- Ganache, p.218
- Sponge, p.84

Choux Paste, p.24

Corn
- Corn and Dill, p.142
- Corn Relish, p.186
- Pudding, p.190

Court-Bouillon, p.10

Couscous, p.18

Crêpes
- Crespelle Gratinate alla Valdostana, p.54

Desserts
- Baked Alaska, p.150
- Black Forest Gâteau, p.84
- Buttermilk-Vanilla Ice Cream, p.218
- Canela Tortilla Stack, p.194
- Caramelized William Pear Tart, p.44
- Chantilly Cream, p.174
- Chantilly Swans, p.174
- Chocolate Grand Marnier Cake, p.62
- Chocolate Rum Ice Cream, p.218
- Chocolate Sponge, p.84
- Choux Paste, p.174
- Classic Cheesecake, p.22
- Custard, Vanilla, p.152
- Drambuie and Coconut Parfait, p.42
- Dried Apple Crisps, p.106
- Ganache, p.218
- Grape Mille-Feuille, p.212
- Ladyfingers, p.128
- Lemon Poppy Seed Bavaroise, p.64
- Meringue, p.150
- Mousse, Grand Marnier, p.62
- Mousse, Lemon, p.64
- Mousse, White Chocolate, p.214
- Mousse, White Chocolate and Tequila, p.192
- Napoleon, p.82
- Opera Cake, p.214
- Pâte Sucrée (Sweet Pastry), p.152
- Profiteroles and Fresh Berries, p.24
- Raspberry Crème Brûlée, p.102
- Rhubarb Custard Tart, p.152
- Royale (Jelly Roll), p.62
- Santa Fe Margarita, p.192
- Strawberry-Cointreau Ice Cream, p.218
- Tarte Tatin, p.106
- Tiramisu, p.130
- Tuiles, p.130, 192
- Vanilla-Cognac Soufflé, p.172
- Vanilla Ice Cream, p.106
- Vanilla Sponge, p.150
- Zabaglione (Sabayon), p.128

Duck
- Canard à l'Orange, p.98
- Gently Smoked Supreme of Duck, p.28

Dumplings, Oriental, p.202

Duxelles, p.210

Eggplant Parmigiana, p.114

Escargots à la Bourguignonne, p.90

Fish
- Baked Flounder Parmentier, p.38
- Branzino Cileno, p.124
- Chili and Cumin-Rubbed Catfish, p.186
- Ketchikan Silver Salmon, p.142
- Poached Weave of Halibut and Salmon, p.144
- Potato-Crusted Shark Filet, p.162
- Sautéed Filet of Zander, p.18
- Seared Ahi Tuna, p.76
- Smoked Copper River Salmon, p.136

Fondant, p.218

Frog Legs (Grenouilles Provençal), p.96

Game
- Old-Fashioned Pot-Roast Buffalo, p.208
- Oven-Roasted Spatchcock, p.148
- Pan-Roasted Venison Loin, p.40
- Rabbit (Sella di Lepre Arrostito), p.118
- Reindeer Chili, p.140
- Royal Pheasant in Pan Juices, p.166
- Venison Marinade, p.40

Lamb
- Rack of Lamb Dijonnaise, p.80

Lemon Cream Sauce, p. 18

Lentils, Braised, p.76

Mango Salsa, p.10

Onion
- Caramelized Onion and Bacon Tart, p.12

Parfait, Drambuie and Coconut, p.42

Pasta
- Asiago Cheese Stuffed Gnocchi, p.204
- Conchiglie alla Campagnola, p.16
- Farfalle alla Rustica, p.34
- Linguine al Pesto alla Moda Ligure, p.74
- Nouilles Façon Cannebière, p.94

Pastry Cream
- Anise, p.82
- Vanilla, p.24

Pâte Brisée, p.221

Pear
- Caramelized William Pear Tart, p.44
- Pear Slaw, p.136

Peas, Creamed, p.220

Pesto, p.74

Polenta, p.96

Pork
- Porc Normande, p.100
- Prosciutto Crudo di Parma, p.112

Potatoes
- Almond Macaire, p.100
- Anna, p.60
- Château, p.170
- Dauphinoise, p.171

Duchesse, p.171
Garlic, Mashed, p.80
Gaufrette, p.40
Mashed, Red Bliss, p.142
Noisette, p.58
Sweet, Glazed, p.219
Sweet, Roasted, p.190
Williams, p.98

Profiteroles and Fresh Berries, p.24

Prosciutto Crudo di Parma, p.112

Pumpernickel, Domino Bread, p.136

Quesadilla, Brie and Papaya, p.180

Quiche
Crawfish Quiche, p.30

Ratatouille, p.58

Red Cabbage, Braised, p.40

Relish
Jalapeño Relish, p.30

Rice
Basmati with Saffron, p.36
Braised Wild Rice, p.148
Jasmine, Saffron Pilaf, p.164
Mexican Dirty Rice, p.188

Risotto al Nero di Seppia, p.124

Roquefort Crust, p.60

Salad
Cabbage Slaw, p.50
Cucumber, p.142
Original Caesar Salad, p.184
Pear Slaw, p.136
Premium Seafood, p.70
Radicchio, Endive and Butter Lettuce, p.14
Tender Baby Spinach, p.158
Warm Grilled Chicken Supreme, p.48

Salsa
Mango, p.10

Sauce
Amaretto, p.218
Anglaise, p.44
Basil Pesto, p.74
Bearnaise, p.170
Béchamel, p.217
Beurre Noisette, p.38
Blueberry Tamarillo, p.82
Bordelaise, p.210
Caesar Dressing, p.184
Café de Paris Butter, p.90
Calvados, p.100
Caramel Apple, p.106
Chive, p.221
Chocolate, p.150
Chocolate-Mocha, p.174
Cooked Rich Tomato, p.217
Corn and Dill, p.142
Cranberry Dressing, p.219
Demi-Glace, p.220
Drawn Butter, p.146
Dried Cranberry with Rum, p.148
Dried Peppers and Whiskey, p.190
Fiery Tomato, p.219
Fresh Tomato, p.114
Ganache, p.218
Giblet Gravy, p.219
Gooseberry, p.40
Grand Marnier, p.172
Grape Pinot Noir, p.212
Herb Butter, p.78
Horseradish Cream, p.217
Kahlúa, p.214
Lemon Cream, p.18
Lemon-Lobster Butter, p.164
Orange Sauce for Duck, p.98
Papaya and Honey, p.42
Papaya Seed Dressing, p.70
Parsley-Basil Oil, p.112
Périgueux, p.166
Red Pepper Jus, p.80
Rémoulade, p.198
Saffron Foam, p.76
Saffron Nage, p.72
Sherry Mousseline, p.36
Spring Leek, p.144
Strawberry Coulis, p.22
Strawberry-Rhubarb Coulis, p.152
Tomato Compote, p.90, 138
Veal, p.60
Whole Grain Mustard and Chives, p.138

Seafood
Alaskan King Crab Legs, p.146
Baked Clams Casino, p.50
Broiled Lobster Tail, p.164
Caribbean Tiger Shrimp Cocktail, p.10
Crawfish Quiche, p.30
Dungeness Crab Cakes, p.138
Gamberi alla Frá Diavolo, p.122
Lobster Thermidor, p.36
Marsala and Shallots, p.126
Nouilles Façon Cannebière, p.94
Premium Seafood and Avocado, p.198
Seafood Potpourri in a Saffron Nage, p.72
Seared Deep Sea Scallops, p.58
Tequila Prawns, p.188
Tian of Premium Seafood and Gin-Cured Salmon, p.70

Soup
Chilled Golden Delicious Apple and Peach, p.32
Chilled Strawberry Cream, p.52
Cream of Porcini and Wild Mushroom, p.160
Double Beef Consommé, p.202
Reindeer Chili, p.140
Rustic Vegetable Minestrone, p.116
Soupe à l'Oignon Gratinée, p.92
Texas Lobster and Black Bean, p.182

Stock
Beef, p.220
Chicken, p.221
Fish, p.220
Lamb Jus, p.219
Lobster, p.220
Turkey, p.221
Veal, p.221
Vegetable, p.221

Stuffing, Bread-Fruit, p.206

Tomato
Clamart, p.170
Compote, p.90
Cooked Rich Tomato Sauce, p.217
Fresh Tomato Sauce, p.114
Sun-Dried Tomato Vinaigrette, p.14

Turkey, Roasted Young Tom, p.206

Veal
Farfalle alla Rustica, p.34
Medallions of Veal Tenderloin, p.60
Vitello allo Scalogno, p.126

Vinaigrette
Cassis Vinaigrette, p.28
Cilantro, p.180
Citrus Vinaigrette, p.48
Red Wine Vinaigrette, p.158
Sun-Dried Tomato Vinaigrette, p.14

BY THE END OF A PANAMA CANAL CROSSING, THE PASSENGERS

ON A SINGLE SHIP WILL HAVE CONSUMED 350,000 POUNDS OF FOOD.